"*Prophetic Forecast* is not just a ⋯ God's prophetic Spirit leading the Body of Chr⋯ Giles penned a relevant resourc⋯ and prophetic insight to see fr⋯ plan of God for the future of t⋯

**Dr. Hakeem Collins**, prophetic voice, international speaker, author of *The Power of Aligning Your Words to God's Will*

"In *Prophetic Forecast*, Joshua Giles skillfully reveals intricate prophetic details for this new era. He also gives the reader insight and encouragement on how to be positioned as a glorious overcomer and frontliner in the midst of all that lies ahead. I highly recommend this book to all who are longing for knowledge, insight and wisdom concerning the future."

**Patricia King**, author, minister, media host

"In *Prophetic Forecast*, Joshua Giles presents a revelatory perspective on a variety of global, societal and church issues. It is sure to challenge believers to pray, hear from heaven and know how to align their hearts and lives."

**Jane Hamon**, apostle, Vision Church @ Christian International; author of *Dreams and Visions* and *Declarations for Breakthrough*

"Whenever someone asks me about trusted prophetic voices today, one of the first people I mention is Joshua Giles. Though he is an emerging prophetic voice to many, his track record has already been established by those of us who have followed his ministry for years. That's why I'm so excited about my dear friend's book *Prophetic Forecast*! This book is fire. Read it, and allow the tools within it to equip you to be the prophetic voice God is calling you to be for your sphere of influence."

**Will Ford**, founder, Dream Stream Company and 818 The Sign; author of *The Dream King*

# PROPHETIC
# FORECAST

# PROPHETIC FORECAST

INSIGHTS FOR NAVIGATING THE FUTURE
TO ALIGN WITH HEAVEN'S AGENDA

## JOSHUA GILES

**Chosen**

a division of Baker Publishing Group
Minneapolis, Minnesota

Published by Chosen Books
11400 Hampshire Avenue South
Minneapolis, Minnesota 55438
www.chosenbooks.com

Chosen Books is a division of
Baker Publishing Group, Grand Rapids, Michigan

Printed in the United States of America

Library of Congress Cataloging-in-Publication Data
Names: Giles, Joshua, 1988– author.
Title: Prophetic forecast : insights for navigating the future to align
  with heaven's agenda / Joshua Giles.
Description: Minneapolis, Minnesota : Chosen Books, a division of Baker Publishing Group,
  [2022]
Identifiers: LCCN 2021051905 | ISBN 9780800762384 (trade paper) | ISBN 9780800762650
  (casebound) | ISBN 9781493435876 (ebook)
Subjects: LCSH: End of the world. | Bible—Prophecies. | Twenty-first
  century—Forecasts—Miscellanea. | Prophecies.
Classification: LCC BT877 .G55 2022 | DDC 236/.9—dc23/eng/20211118
LC record available at https://lccn.loc.gov/2021051905

Cover design by Bill Johnson

Baker Publishing Group publications use paper produced from sustainable forestry practices and post-consumer waste whenever possible.

22  23  24  25  26  27  28      8  7  6  5  4  3  2

I give all glory and honor to God for this phenomenal opportunity to write and to share His heart with those of you who read this book. I love You, Jesus, with my whole heart and will serve you for the rest of my life!

I would also like to dedicate this book to those people who over the years have consistently supported the vision and ministry that God placed in me. What an adventurous and amazing journey it is!

# CONTENTS

# FOREWORD

And when they had prayed, the place was shaken where they were assembled together; and they were all filled with the Holy Ghost, and they spake the word of God with boldness.

Acts 4:31 KJV

Believers in the early Church prayed in such a manner that the physical ground beneath their feet was shaken! I believe that this was not only a physical, but also a spiritual shaking. Recently as I was in prayer, I heard the Lord say that the tectonic plates of the modern prophetic movement are shifting. God is exposing new voices, new vessels and is releasing His fresh breath upon new moves. A glorious transformation is taking place, and we get to be on the front lines of it.

The aim of the prophetic is to capture and release the mind and heart of God. It is a combination of inside information along with the power to bring about remarkable transformation. In many ways, the prophetic is as much about movement and reformation as it is insight. Prophetic words cause stuck things to move. Prophetic worship causes divine release to happen. Prophetic intercession causes the breaking forth of waves of God's glory in the earth.

We are standing at the dawn of a stunning new day. The earth is literally groaning for the release of bold sons and daughters! There are new moves to be birthed and exploits to unfold. We must navigate these times of unprecedented challenge and opportunity with the wisdom of God. It is the role of the prophets to skillfully release the red-hot word of the Lord to us with no agenda but heaven's.

I believe that there is a daring new breed of pioneer arising to take God's voice to every nation, every corner of the globe and every system of our society. God wants to speak to the leaders of government, entertainment, industry, education, health care and all other human systems. He is sending those who have been alone with Him to release His Word into the earth, with miraculous results.

Joshua Giles is on the front lines of this emerging move. He is an accurate voice, with strong spiritual sight and potent building capacity. He speaks the language of heaven with a remarkable accuracy to warn and forecast regarding the things to come. The pages of this book are both timely and timeless. You will receive inside information that is relevant for this exact moment, but you will also receive the teaching and instruction that you need for every season as a believer who is hungry to hear and know the Father. Grab your notebook and prepare to be enlightened as you dive deep into this prophetic masterpiece!

Ryan LeStrange, author, *Breaking Curses*; founder, Ryan LeStrange Ministries and AtlHub

# ACKNOWLEDGMENTS

To my parents, who raised me in the nurture and admonition of the Lord, thank you and I love you immensely. Mom, Debra Giles, you helped me develop my spiritual gifts as a young child and taught me about the prophetic, business and life. It was your tenacity and strength that fueled me to reach for more. Your love and support have sustained me. Dad, Tyrone Giles, you taught me to study the Word of God and about the necessity of fasting and prayer. I also appreciate the support of my family unit (you know who you are). You have been there through the mountains and valleys. Now it's our time to walk in generational blessings.

To my spiritual parents, Bishop Tudor Bismark and Pastor Chi Chi Bismark, your impact and impartation have changed my life. I haven't been the same since coming into covenant with you. Bishop Tudor, your personal mentorship, teaching and example of love have shown me how to be a leader and a man of integrity. I will always honor you!

To Pastor Runette C. Jones, you have been a mentor in prophetic ministry since I was a young child, and you are one of the most accurate prophets I know. I honor your anointing and thank you for pouring into my life!

To the late Dr. Sheila Spencer, she accomplished so much in her short time here on earth. She will forever be remembered for her integrity and as a pioneer in ministry.

To my committed and hardworking core team, you are the best! All of you serve so faithfully, and I pray God rewards you exponentially for investing your time. James Bolden and Giordano Madison, thank you for sacrificing so much to see the vision come to pass. I am grateful for those of you who work alongside me, both near and far. We have traveled to nations, served communities and shared the message of Jesus Christ. We have more work to do!

To Kingdom Embassy Worship Center, you are my tribe, my people, and I love you. Thank you for the privilege of doing life together.

Lastly, I would like to thank Baker Publishing Group and the Chosen Books team for all the hard work, strategy and care you have put into bringing this project to a successful completion. You gave my voice a home, and you pushed me as a writer. Because of you, I am confident in the quality of this project. I appreciate you for making this an exciting and enjoyable experience.

# INTRODUCTION

This is one of the most unusual books that the Holy Spirit has inspired me to write. I would even say that it is more of a prophecy—a foretelling of what is to come. Furthermore, it gives insight into what is happening right now in the world and in the Body of Christ. The prophetic instructions I give here are written to encourage you, empower you and at times warn you of impending disaster so that you might be able to adequately prepare for what is ahead. In this book, through prophetic insight we will travel to the future and catch a glimpse of what is coming so that we can pray, align with God's agenda and plan with biblical strategy. That is the purpose of the prophetic dimension. The prophetic dimension can transport you ahead and give you the advantage of knowing what to do.

To go forward into the future, I will have to take you back in time to three very timely and uncanny prophecies that the Lord gave me. I spoke them publicly at my church in Minnesota, with several hundred members in attendance. They are well documented and recorded. First, on December 6, 2015,

God gave me a prophecy about a rare virus that would come. Each year, I typically do one major prophetic gathering on a Sunday at my church. I do these special meetings only as the Holy Spirit leads. In this particular service, as we were in the midst of spontaneous worship and praise, the Spirit of prophecy came upon me in a strong and intensified way. I began to speak with a boldness and clarity that was not my own:

> I see a new strain of a virus that will come. It's so rare that the doctors won't know what it is. Many will be confused as to what it is. At first some doctors and others will say, "Is it the flu or not?" But it's going to be so rare. I hear them saying it's mimicking other viruses and diseases. God says it's going to be so rare, that they will have two tests to verify what it is. It will target the breathing and the respiratory system. God says that we must pray now and cover the immune systems of ourselves and family members!

The Lord emphasized again to me that this would be a rare virus we had never seen before. As I spoke these words, our Sunday morning congregation was already in prayer mode, although some seemed startled by the directness and type of prophecy the Lord was releasing. They had heard me release many prophecies before, but this was quite different. Everyone stood and started praying. As we engaged in intercession, the Lord told me that this virus was man-made and would come from a lab. Who could know that Covid-19 would come to the shores of America just four years later? Only God could know. The Lord allowed me to know that this would be the first of many other pathogens that would affect the world's population in the future. He strongly comforted my heart to understand that we were not to panic or worry, because He would protect His people.

The second prophecy I will share was given a few years ago, but it speaks to what is happening even now. On September 4, 2019, God gave me a word concerning a major disruption coming, but He reiterated that at the same time, the gifts of the Spirit would intensify. I gave this word on an ordinary Bible study night. There was nothing super special about that day. I had just arrived back in the United States a few days before. I had traveled to minister in Athens, Greece, and then Tel Aviv and Jerusalem, Israel. I experienced amazing encounters with the Lord on this ministry trip. I ministered to and prophesied over two ambassadors who had come for a private meeting. Then by the grace of God, I had the privilege of ministering to the cabinet of a high-profile prime minister. When I got back to the States, I was tired but still ignited and stirred from all that God had done. In the middle of my teaching, the Holy Spirit so graciously took over the Bible study lesson. A strong Spirit of prophecy dropped down on me. Immediately I began to prophesy:

> The Lord says, *You will need wisdom to navigate the times that are ahead. For the times and season are beginning to change.* And the Lord says, *You will see great powers shift among you. You will see great powers in the world begin to shift. That's why I am releasing another dimension and dispensations of My spiritual gifts,* says God. *My gifts are being poured out on My people in a greater measure. For there will be need of them, and you will be needed in the times that are ahead.*
>
> I hear and see a collapse in the Spirit, and the Lord says, *As we step over into 2020, it shall mark a day and a time of a collapse. Not just in America, but the world! For*

*prophets have prophesied that it shall come, and prophets have said that it would happen. You will see a domino effect go throughout the world. It will start in the financial industries, and it will hit every system, says God. This will be the beginning of a global reset.*

Then the Lord finished by saying something exciting: *At the time, you will see the start of one of the greatest revivals that the earth has ever seen.* Even as I write these words, we are seeing this prophecy unfold before our eyes.

Then came a third prophetic word. God spoke to me again about a global reset. While ministering in a New Year's Eve service at my church on December 31, 2019, the Holy Spirit said, *Tell the people that you are about to see a global reset in the world.* He said that the reset would hit every industry, system and aspect of society. In that prophecy, the Holy Spirit said that 2020 would mark the beginning of a period of collapse in the world and a global economic decline. Every system would be reset. And then we would see a resurgence. I gave this prophecy at the end of 2019 and then began teaching on the reset and how 2020 would be the vehicle that would bring us into a new era.

Looking back on 2020, it is clear that it was the year that changed the world. Covid-19 was a major disruptor of society. That virus was the transportation bringing us into a new epoch in the world. By the leading of the Spirit, I shared that word concerning a global reset for many months, to thousands of people both in services and online. God had given me that phrase *a global reset* before it became commonplace to use it. I had never heard that phrase before the Lord spoke it to me; however, it sums up the place that the world has been in for some time now.

I am sharing these three previous prophetic words to let you know that nothing—and I mean absolutely nothing—catches God by surprise. He is aware of what will happen before it unfolds. He is so omniscient that He even knows what we will think before it enters into our minds. God is amazing and full of compassion toward us, that He would send us accurate words to help us navigate the future. The prophetic insights throughout this book are meant to point our attention to Jesus. As Revelation 19:10 so powerfully states, "the testimony of Jesus is the spirit of prophecy."

# 1

# Architects of the Future

I have also spoken by the prophets, and have multiplied
visions; I have given symbols through the witness of the
prophets.

Hosea 12:10

The future belongs to those who have vision—the spiritual
eyes to see it. The Bible is laced with concepts, imagery and
prophecies of the future. Throughout the ages, people have
searched to know the future and to understand it before it
occurs. Many have felt that to know or understand the future
would unlock their dreams and help them gain success in
life. Although capturing the future has profound blessings,
to know it is also a burden because you are faced with the
challenge of what to do with what you know. The Bible
reveals that God ordained and called some to be prophets
(see Ephesians 4:11). Prophets are those who speak on behalf of God in the earth. There are different levels or ranks

of prophets. Some can walk so closely with God that they speak *as God's voice* in the earth.

Amos 3:7 explains, "Surely the Lord GOD does nothing, unless He reveals His secret to His servants the prophets." Prophets are given the rare gift to know the mysteries of time and the secrets of heaven. The Lord may reveal His heart, meaning what He desires to come into being. He may also reveal what actually will happen in the future, although that outcome may not be His desire. God put spiritual laws in place that govern our world, and one supreme law is that He gave humanity dominion over the earth (see Genesis 1:26–28). There are times throughout history when God has intervened in the affairs of people, and sometimes He still does, but generally people's decisions influence their environment. This is key for us to understand, because due to people's choices, many outcomes will occur that are not the plan of God.

I came to the realization that God had called me as a prophet at a very young age, because I would have dreams and visions concerning family or life events. The events I would dream or the visions I would see would happen exactly as I had seen them. Around the age of seven, my experiences led me to go to my church leaders and tell them about the things I had been seeing and hearing. These leaders affirmed the calling that was upon my life. Later, I began hearing the audible voice of the Lord. God would speak to me concerning personal, community or even world events. I would share these things in church services, and they would come to pass.

I have been operating in public prophetic ministry for over eighteen years. I have had the rare opportunity to prophesy to heads of state, government leaders, well-known individuals and the like. Throughout my years of ministry, I have found that God loves communicating with His people. He desires to connect with us on a personal level. It is hard to fathom, but He loves us so much! The future belongs to those who love God and are called for His purpose.

We all carry the future within us; most of us are just not aware of it. Even if you are not a prophet, the prophetic essence of God dwells within the hearts of human beings. Ecclesiastes 3:11 says, "He has made everything beautiful in its time. Also, He has put eternity in their hearts, except that no one can find out the work that God does from beginning to end." God has placed eternity in people's hearts. What does this mean? The word *eternity* in the original Hebrew translation of this verse means the future.[1] God has placed the future in your heart. Your heart is the central organ that pumps blood throughout your entire body. This means that the future is coursing through your veins. You are an eternal being having this natural experience of living life on earth.

This is why we are able to call those things forth that are not, as though they are (see Romans 4:17). As a prophet, I *foretell*, which is to declare things before they occur. I also *forthtell*, however, which is to speak God's words in order to create something that is not currently in existence. Every prophetic believer has this same ability. Secular societies have taken this ancient biblical principle and currently call it affirmations and manifesting what they desire. But this principle has its roots in the Word of God. John 15:7 states, "If you abide in Me, and My words abide in you, you will ask what you desire, and it shall be done for you." If you are aligned with God and His agenda for you, if you have true relationship with Him, then you will call things forth and they will be done.

## The Spiritual Side of "Futures Studies"

To know that you are carrying the future is an amazing thing. In the fields of sociology, technology and even theology there is a subject matter called *futures studies*. In the secular world, futures studies is used as a tool for forecasting, tracking environmental trends and exploring how people will live and work in the future. On the spiritual side of this, the Holy Spirit guides us on what is to come in the future. I want to use the practical example of futures studies to show you how to navigate the future that you see spiritually.

There are four main approaches to futures studies, or foresight. They are the *predictive approach*, the *interpretive approach*, the *critical approach* and the *participatory action learning approach*. These all have both secular and spiritual applications. Let's look at each of them individually and talk about how they can relate to your study of the future in the spiritual.

### The Predictive Approach

First, there is the predictive approach. Throughout time, people have tried every way possible, from astrology to New Age practices, to predict the future. These methods have proven deficient. Although some of the information gleaned from them can be accurate, they have lacked the fullness of the Spirit of truth. The Holy Spirit in Scripture is called the Ancient of Days. He is known as the Spirit of wisdom in Proverbs chapter 8, and He is the Spirit of truth. He was there before the foundations of the world were perfectly fashioned. It is only through Him that we access eternity and heaven's mysteries.

In our modern times, academia seeks to predict the future by studying the trends and using systematic models that can forecast possible outcomes. In prophetic ministry, the predictive aspect of foretelling does not use computer systems or man-made tools; rather, we can predict outcomes based on the Holy Spirit's leading. The predictive aspect is part of the prophetic function, but it is not the central aspect of it. To predict is to say what will be a consequence of something or what will happen in the future. Because God is omniscient, He knows the future, and His foresight is 100 percent accurate.

In Scripture, God gave His predictive counsel to people through four specific modes: *dreams*, *visions*, *prophecy* and *perception*. These are four vehicles that carry prophets and prophetic people into the future. Let's discuss these in more detail for a moment. *Dreams* are an essential way that God communicates. The Bible is filled with colorful, expressive and prophetic dreams. Some scholars believe that one third of the Bible is written about dreams or their interpretation. Why would God communicate through dreams, and why is the Bible decorated with them? This makes perfect sense, because sleep studies have shown that one third of a human life is spent asleep. If God cannot get through to us when we are awake, then when we are asleep is an opportune time for Him to speak. In the sleep state, the mind is unconscious and there is nothing hindering spiritual communication. The Bible says it this way:

> For God does speak—now one way, now another—though no one perceives it. In a dream, in a vision of the night, when deep sleep falls on people as they slumber in their beds, he may speak in their ears and terrify them with warnings, to turn them from wrongdoing and keep them from pride, to preserve them from the pit, their lives from perishing by the sword.
>
> Job 33:14–18 NIV

*Visions* are similar to dreams, except that they occur when a person is awake. Bible verses are also filled with visions. A vision can show up as simply as a picture in the mind, or as vividly as a scene of a movie playing out in front of you.

I can remember having one of my first visions when I was much younger. It was so real that I thought I was actually seeing a certain person in front of me. Throughout my years of prophetic ministry, I have seen many visions of the future, which I have shared publicly, and which have come to pass. I believe that you can walk so closely with the Spirit of God that seeing in the spiritual realm becomes a regular part of your life. Having a vision does not have to be a deep or spooky experience. The Holy Spirit is so real, however, and the spirit world is just as real as this natural world. Actually, everything in this natural world only exists because of the spiritual world.

One of the most intriguing expressions of God is *prophecy*. Prophecy has existed throughout time. It has been recorded throughout every generation and in every earthly age or period of time. Authentic prophecy has its origin in the Bible. True prophecy comes from God. He speaks to those whom He chooses, and we relay it to others. Yes, God is still speaking today, and He desires to communicate with you. The voice of the Lord can be as small as a thought or a whisper, or as loud as thunder. Although I will be releasing prophecy throughout this entire book, my goal is also to unlock a deeper prophetic dimension within you. You may or may not already be identified as a prophet as you read this. If you are not, it is important to realize that just because you are not a prophet does not mean God cannot speak to you.

In Numbers 11 in the Old Testament, God told Moses to gather seventy elders whom He would then place His Spirit upon. God's Spirit came down upon them like a cloud, and they began to prophesy. In verse 29, Moses said, "I wish that all the Lord's people were prophets and that the Lord would put his Spirit on them!" (NIV). In 1 Corinthians 14:5 in the New Testament, the apostle Paul echoed the same sentiments as Moses: "I would like every one of you to speak in tongues, but I would rather have you prophesy. The one who prophesies is greater than the one who speaks in tongues, unless someone interprets, so that the church may be edified" (NIV). Through these verses, we can gather that God desires all His people to be prophetic types. He desires that all would prophesy and carry the essence of a prophet. Prophets are stewards of the mysteries of God. And God wants you to know His mysteries and to hear His secret thoughts about the future. This does not mean that every believer holds the *office* of a prophet—meaning someone who is specifically called as a prophet as part of the fivefold ministry (according to Ephesians 4:11–12). Yet all believers carry a prophetic essence. You are God's prophetic people.

The last vehicle for communicating the future is *perception*. Scripture relates instances where someone would perceive what God wanted or what would happen. Perception is spiritual sight or vision. It is in the realm of supernatural knowledge; this is when you know what will happen in the future because God has put it in your heart. There was no audible voice, just a spiritual perceiving or knowing. We see one example of this vehicle or mode at work in 2 Samuel 5:12 (KJV): "And David perceived that the LORD had established him king over Israel, and that he had exalted his kingdom for his people Israel's sake." When God does not speak audibly concerning a matter, and when there is no dream or vision, there is still spiritual perception. There are times in your life when you will perceive what your next move should be. This is an assurance and a knowing that can only come from God.

### The Interpretive Approach

Going back to the idea of futures studies, the second approach is interpretive. This approach is not based on forecasting, but on contrasting competing ideas or images of the future. Spiritually speaking, there are infinite futures for your personal life. Your outcome is in part controlled by your decisions. Your decisions determine your destiny. God gives you options. He will never force you to choose a specific path, although He makes known to you His will for your life. Your future is in your willingness to surrender to His will.

In huge decisions that directly affect your destiny, such as your career, whom you marry or what you do with your life, God must be consulted. You must even acknowledge Him in the small decisions. When a decision does not directly affect your destiny, however, you get to choose. God is less concerned with the kind of car you drive and more concerned with the condition of your soul. When it comes to decisions He has placed in your hands, He has given you creativity, innovation and an imagination so that—combined with the wisdom of God—you can dream, you can envision and you can choose the path you will take.

A core part of the prophetic dimension is the ability to create the future that you see in your heart. You do this with your thinking, your decisions and your words. This is why repentance, or a change of mind, is so important. When our mind is renewed through the Word and Spirit of God, our thinking follows. Then we speak the words of God.

Hebrews 11:3 says, "By faith we understand that the worlds were framed by the word of God, so that the things which are seen were not made of things which are visible." Words come from the invisible realm—the spiritual realm (the heart and mind). The example in this verse shows that words frame worlds. There are infinite worlds in the universe, and God is the author of all of them. He gave us that same creative power to frame our world. What we speak determines the infrastructure and the framework for the reality that we live in. Choose your words carefully because they create your reality. This is not to be confused with a simple and faulty "name it and claim it" theology, of course. But when your heart and behavior align with God's Word, you can speak what God has said and it will manifest in your life.

### The Critical and Participatory Action Approaches

The third approach in futures studies is called the critical approach. It is the concept that asks who benefits from the realization of certain futures. And the fourth approach is participatory action learning. You see this fourth approach used with stakeholders in a company who are developing their future based on their own research and assumptions.

These two approaches are not as applicable on the spiritual side as the first two, but through them we can still derive some prophetic symbolism. You are the stakeholder of your destiny and future. You benefit from investing God's Word into your soul. Without understanding the importance of your partnership with the Holy Spirit, you will live beneath your privilege as a believer.

Although these various approaches are the concepts that drive futures studies in the secular world, they differ in ways from discerning, predicting and pursuing your future in the spiritual. In its simplest form, a prophetic forecast is capturing the mind of God for your life and destiny. It is carrying the future and speaking what the Spirit of God says. In the same way that meteorologists forecast the weather for the week, we can discern our times spiritually. In Matthew 16:2–3, Jesus scolded the Pharisees and Sadducees for their ability to predict the weather and not the times:

When it is evening you say, "It will be fair weather, for the sky is red"; and in the morning, "It will be foul weather today, for the sky is red and threatening." Hypocrites! You know how to discern the face of the sky, but you cannot discern the signs of the times.

Discerning the times is an extraordinary gift, yet it is uncommon because many believers are unaware of how to access their prophetic nature. The future resides within (see Luke 17:21) and can only be unlocked by understanding the Kingdom of God and embracing the power of the Holy Spirit.

## Where the Spirit Is about to Go

Recorded in Ezekiel chapter 1 is a vision Ezekiel had of a massive whirlwind with an expansive cloud. Out of the cloud came lightning and a deep bronze color. Then there emerged four living creatures. Each of them had four faces and four wings. These living creatures moved so fast, like a flash of lightning. Ezekiel also saw in the vison four wheels, one beside each cherub. It appeared to him that there was a wheel in the middle of a wheel, and that along the wheels' rims they were full of eyes. One of the wheels was upon the earth, while the others were in other heavenly domains. Ezekiel saw this massive, otherworldly glory system moving as a heavenly vehicle at the direction of the Spirit of God: "Wherever the spirit was about to go, they would go in that direction" (verse 20 NASB).

To forecast the future is to discern the way that the Spirit of God is about to move. It is discerning the shifts and changes that are coming in the wind and moving in that direction. Like Ezekiel's vision, we must be so in step with the Holy Spirit that we are sensitive to His every movement. We cannot get stuck where God was in a previous season. We cannot be stuck in what God was doing or moving in before. We have to be so aligned with Him that we pick up on where He is about to go.

To prophesy is to hear, capture and proclaim what God is about to do. Not only can you hear what God is going to do; in the Spirit you can be carried there. You can live in a future that others have not yet seen. You can dwell in a dimension that has not yet manifested in reality. Through the prophetic dimension, you become an architect of the future. You build your tomorrow with the words that you speak prophetically today!

Prophetic forecasting gives us the advantage of knowing what will happen so that we can plan, prepare and navigate the times ahead.

## YOUR PROPHETIC FORECAST

In this new era we have entered, God is doing a new thing. It is imperative that you are sensitive to the moving of the Holy Spirit and what He is intending to birth through you. You will be challenged to let go of the old in order to grasp the new thing. Jeremiah 29:11 reminds us that God's plans toward us are intentional and by design: "For I know the thoughts that I think toward you, says the LORD, thoughts of peace and not of evil, to give you a future and a hope." He already has the future mapped out. You just simply have to trust Him so you can walk in the fullness of His plan and purpose for your life.

It is essential to seek God, align with His agenda and know His heart. In the prophetic activation exercise that follows, answer these questions in your personal prayer time. (You will find a similar "Your Prophetic Forecast" section near the end of each chapter. The questions I ask, or the takeaways I provide, will help you reflect on and apply what you have just read. Also be sure to read the "Prophetic Hope" section that concludes each chapter. It will give you inspiration and encouragement to forge ahead with God's plan for your life.)

1. What do you see or hear spiritually concerning your future?
2. What is God saying to you about the new era?
3. How can you align with heaven's agenda for your life?
4. What area of ministry are you called to serve in?
5. What are your short-term goals for working toward the future you want to see?
6. What are your long-term goals for working toward the future you want to see?
7. What are you leaving behind and letting go of?

 **PROPHETIC HOPE**

God wants to partner with you to construct the future that you desire, based on the foundation of His Word and principles. By embracing and believing the Word of God, you can build a better future. Your voice is a powerful tool to activate your best future, which is God's will for your life. When you prophesy and declare God's Word, you give His ideas, plans and purposes permission to live in your world. Never stop speaking what God has said, because your words create reality.

## 2

# A New Era

His mercy is from age to age to those who fear Him.

Luke 1:50 NABRE

We are on the cusp of major change in the world. Life as we know it will be completely different in the months and years to come. I heard the Spirit of God say to me,

> *The earth is entering into a new era. The way that the world operates and the way that you are used to conducting life is being rearranged and reordered. Many within the Church will fight it because they do not understand it, but I am allowing this transition as time is giving birth to a new order in the earth.*

I was confounded by this prophecy, and it rocked me to my core as I continued to seek God for what He meant. I have come to realize that the world has gone through many different ages or epochs in time, all leading to the fulfillment of biblical prophecy. At the transition of each age, the world experiences tumult or disasters. Each age proclaims a new dispensation of time. Let's take a look at some of the many ages[1] that the world has gone through:

- Prehistoric
  - » Paleolithic
  - » Mesolithic
  - » Neolithic
  - » Chalcolithic (Copper Age)
- Ancient History—civilizations and regions that had developed a writing system and continued the advancement of technology
  - » Bronze Age
  - » Iron Age
- Late Middle Ages
  - » Renaissance
- Early Modern History
- Modern History
  - » Industrial Age (1760–1970)
  - » Machine Age (1880–1945)
    - Age of Oil (1901–present)
    - Jet Age (1940s)
  - » Atomic Age (1945–present)
  - » Space Age (1957–present)
  - » Information Age (1970–present)

I shared this example of the ages just so that you can see how much the world has changed over time. There was a time in the 1800s that you would have had to ride a horse and buggy just to see your family in another state. Now, without a second thought you can jump on a virtual call or video. With each progressing age, time has been accelerated. What would have taken weeks, days or hours can now be done in seconds and milliseconds. This is due to the increase of knowledge and technology. It is clear that each age brings about massive change. In the prophecy, however, God did not say we were just going into another age. He said a *new era*. Webster's dictionary tells us that an *era* is a period identified by a prominent feature.[2] An era is a merging and intersecting of overlapping ages.

We will see a new era of leadership arise in the world. There is a changing of the guard occurring even now, as I write this. Those who have occupied forefront positions in industries, governments and even communities are being rearranged. The new era of leadership will be a time of transition like that of Moses and Joshua in the Bible. It was always the plan of the Lord to bring Moses into the land of promise, yet God was more concerned with the heart and method of leadership than He was about the face of leadership. So many people have glorified the face—meaning the personality, look and style of leadership—until they have forgotten the most important component, the heart. At a desperate time in Israel's transition, when the people needed water, God instructed Moses to speak to the rock:

> Then the Lord spoke to Moses, saying, "Take the rod; you and your brother Aaron gather the congregation together. Speak to the rock before their eyes, and it will yield its water; thus you shall bring water for them out of the rock, and give drink to the congregation and their animals."
>
> Numbers 20:7–8

Instead of speaking to the rock, Moses seemed to act out of frustration. He called the congregation rebels and struck the rock twice. Afterward, water came out the rock abundantly and the people drank, but God was not pleased with Moses. At the time, Moses was the epitome of leadership. He had previously had a radical transformation period in the desert and a supernatural encounter with God manifesting in a burning bush. Moses risked so much to be raised up as the deliverer of Israel. He dealt with immense pressure and warfare against him just for obeying God. Why would he get all the way to this point in his life and Israel's history and disobey God? Numbers 20:12 says, "Then the Lord spoke to Moses and Aaron, 'Because you did not believe Me, to hallow Me in the eyes of the children of Israel, therefore you shall not bring this assembly into the land which I have given them.'" The Bible indicates that Moses did not believe.

Wow, that is hard to even fathom, that Moses did not believe God. Let's look at the word *believe* from the Hebrew perspective. The Hebrew word for believe is *'āman*. It means to build up or support, to foster as a parent, to trust. Now that we understand the meaning of *believe* in Hebrew, to support or trust, it is clear that God was looking for Moses to support His decision and to trust His plan.

In order to lead effectively, leaders must support the decisions of God. The best spiritual leaders are not those who have the best ideas. The best spiritual leaders are those who have a listening ear to hear God speak in the whisper. This sometimes requires following God blindly. Moses knew all of this, but in that moment of frustration he chose to abandon God's decision and carry out his own.

The interesting part of this story is that God had instructed Moses many years before, in a similar crisis at the beginning of the Israelites' wilderness journey, to strike a rock in order to bring forth water. Why would God tell

Moses to strike a rock at one point and then to speak to a rock at another? These two actions represent different styles of leadership. The children of Israel had spent roughly four hundred years in a system of slavery. During that period, their taskmasters would oftentimes strike them to make them obey. In other words, their overseers would use brute force. That brutish style of leadership had been deeply ingrained in Israel as a form used on those who would resist. But the Lord was intending to change the culture and nature of Israel. To do this properly, He had to change the method of leadership they were accustomed to. They had to see that it was not necessary to be subjected to brute force to obey. All God should have had to do was speak to them. When He spoke, the people should have heard Him and obeyed. He was shifting Israel from striking to voice command.

## Emerging Leadership in the New Era

The Holy Spirit spoke to me concerning the change in leadership in the Church globally. Over the next decade, we will see the pulpits in the Church in America and in the nations of the world change rapidly. (I will go into more detail on this in chapter 12, "Changing of the Guard.") Some leaders will pass the baton, while other leaders will step into other capacities. There will be an emergence of new leaders taking the forefront. It is not about age, but vision. There are many who have already been leading, but in diminished capacities. They have been on the backside of the desert, like David, tending the sheep. Those who are faithful and who carry the heart of God will experience promotion. Their spheres of influence will expand, their voices will rise and they will attract the resources they need to carry out God's plan.

In this new era, some Church leaders will be demoted because of their disobedience and hearts that have drifted from God. Romans 11:29 reveals that gifts and callings are without repentance. One translation says they are irrevocable. This means that God will never take a spiritual gift back that He has given you. These leaders who are demoted due to disobedience will not lose their callings, but their influence will diminish greatly, and others will fill their seats of power.

Then there are those leaders who have served well. They will be given double honor. The Lord will move some of them laterally into other assignments. Others among them who have labored for many years and have grown tired will transition to heavenly promotion, going home to be with the Lord. These changes will happen so swiftly that it will mark a period in history for the Church globally.

I also saw in a vision many heads of major Fortune 500 companies no longer occupying their positions. This has already begun to happen, but many leaders in the business world will step down abruptly as there is a reordering of industries and corporations, and some will be removed. We are quickly being ushered into a new era of innovation and fresh ideas. Within this period of time, some of the most revolutionary inventions and modifications will emerge in the world. We will see many new modes and platforms for getting the message of the Gospel out everywhere. (We will talk more about this in chapter 8, "Technology Resurgence.") God will use these innovations to reach a new generation that does not know Him. For this reason, we as believers must embrace the changes quickly in order to be part of the next move of God and awakening in the earth.

## The Resilient Church

Through it all, the Church of the Lord Jesus Christ will grow stronger and stronger as the remnant invades the systems of this world. The amazing thing about God's chosen people, His Church, is that we have survived every kingdom, government and dynasty since the Church's inception. The Church is the most resilient and powerful entity on the face of this earth. We bear the identity and seal of Christ. We are not afraid of the new era that is upon us; rather, we are running toward it!

The end of an eon and an epoch is already upon us. The world as we know it has ended. The end of the age is signaling the beginning of a new era. They are one and the same. The end of the age is not upon us due to the entrance of the Covid-19 pandemic that took the world by storm in 2020, or due to the economic shaking that rippled throughout the world. The shift in the world has been trumpeted by the changing time on God's calendar. Because of this, there will be an uptick of evil in the earth. Evil will try to fight God's agenda, but it will not prevail. Nevertheless, I must share the following prophetic words so that you will be aware of Satan's devices against God's people.

### *Prophecy of Rising Deception and a False Christianity*

The Spirit of God showed me that we will see a great compromise that will emerge in mainstream churches throughout the United States and in other nations. Governments will seek to have its hands on the steering wheel of the Church. And in the vision God is giving me, I see this secret meeting that will occur between key pastors and leaders of large congregations and those who run my country. In the vision, this meeting is taking place behind closed doors, confidentially—with some attending virtually and some in person. Tenets or points are being given in the meeting that every leader is expected to share with his or her respective congregation. Some of these points are regulations regarding the health crisis, while others promote a gospel of inclusion. Although some Church leaders will not take the bait, there are others who will.

This collaboration between those in high places who run the country and faith leaders will be a demonic alliance designed to push a secular humanistic agenda. These influential pastors will be pressured not to preach against sin. The Spirit of God says,

> *This will be the emergence of the antichrist spirit in a way that the earth has never seen. Many have expected this antichrist spirit to come from those within the world, but no, it shall come from within those who call themselves the Church. They will succumb to the spirit of another Jesus. For it is not Me.*

This will be a dangerous time for the Western Church, where the spirit of compromise will have gained a foothold. A false Christianity will expand that has the image of Christ, but not the likeness. It will have the form of godliness, but will deny the power of God from operating within (see 2 Timothy 3:1–5).

One of the major battles that the true Church of Jesus Christ will have to fight is with the spirit of religion. In this new era, you will see the antichrist spirit arise from some of those who call themselves the Church. This beast will call itself the Church, too, but it will be a mutant of politics, religious features and the idolizing of self. It will promote motivational speaking over the Word of God. It will be like a state-run church. In this prophecy is a warning for those who name the name of Christ to hold fast to His Word. Preach the whole Gospel and the truth. Do not compromise or give in to the spirit of religion.

### Prophecy of New and Engineered Pathogens

In the coming years, new pathogens and mutated viruses will emerge. I see one in particular that will arise, and it will be worse than Covid-19. At that time, panic will ensue as people will say and fear that Covid is back with a vengeance.

Some of these new viruses that emerge will be engineered in laboratories. Some will be weaponized, and others will be used to usher the world into a new system and order. Vaccination centers will be the norm. The Spirit of God showed me that the day will come when yearly vaccinations for variants will become commonplace for the majority of the world's population.

Although vaccinations have been part of the world for many decades, those coming may be very different. I saw a vision of scientists integrating vaccine formulations with technology—a technology that will reside inside the human body and could be used for tracing, monitoring vitals and surveilling. It will likely be monetized and, in turn, give birth to a multibillion-dollar subcategory of the hybrid medical-tech industry.

 ## YOUR PROPHETIC FORECAST

The new era will bring about changes in your personal life. It is imperative that you remain adaptable as the world system shifts into this new epoch. You must position yourself for the shift. New gatekeepers of organizations, communities, cities and regions will emerge. You may be one whom the Lord handpicks and selects to serve for His glory. How can you prepare to align yourself with the agenda of God in this new era? Here are some key things you can do, beginning right now:

1. Increase your knowledge base and always remain a student. The changes that are coming will be difficult for those who are unwilling to be teachable.

2. Prepare to learn new things and shed the old wineskin. God is a God of the new. He gives you the ability to reinvent, recreate and relaunch.

3. Be open to the new directives, instructions and mandates from God in this season.

4. Reevaluate your focus and determine the important things that you should give your time to in this new era.

5. Rediscover your passion for serving and ask the Lord to show you people whom you are assigned to help and pour into.

6. Shore up your biblical foundation to withstand the winds of doctrine that will blow.

7. Increase your spiritual appetite to consume more of the Word of God.

 **PROPHETIC HOPE**

In spite of the changes you see around you, God is unchanging. In Malachi 3:6 (KJV) He states, "I am the LORD, I change not." Although the new era will involve many swift changes and winding paths, your steps have already been ordered by the Lord because you are the righteousness of God in Christ Jesus. The more you trust in God, the more you will experience His peace that surpasses all understanding. The more you build your faith in Him, the more you will see and know His extraordinary love, protection and comfort. This new era will be the adventure of a lifetime, as you walk closely with the Holy Spirit!

3

# A Shaking Is Here

For this is what the LORD of Heaven's Armies says: In just a
little while I will again shake the heavens and the earth, the
oceans and the dry land.

Haggai 2:6 NLT

A few years ago, I went to Egypt with a very small team. I
had been connected with a pastor of a Coptic church there
where they were dealing with great persecution in a specific
area. I thought I was going there for one thing, but the Lord
was allowing me to go to learn many other lessons. From
the moment I landed, everything seemed out of place and
chaotic. I was used to being in the kind of conditions you
find in developing nations, so that did not bother me. I was
held up at customs, and at first was not allowed to enter the
country. I noticed that we were the only Americans in the
line. I was told I would have to pay extra money to get in.
*Okay*, I thought to myself, *if that's required*.

Finally, after getting through the ordeal at airport customs, we jumped into a car with a cab driver who would take us to the hotel. Of course, in places like this, traffic can be hectic. On our way there we were almost run off the road by huge trucks. Needless to say, I was relieved when we made it to the hotel. Although the whole trip was memorable, it seemed as though we ran into disruptions at every turn.

After finally completing my ministry schedule in Egypt and just before flying off to Israel, I decided to go see the pyramids of Giza. I am a lover of history, and I thought, *There's no way I can come to Egypt and not see the pyramids.* The visit was one of the most amazing experiences, but while standing there, out of the blue I said to my team, "It would be horrible to be caught in a dust storm here."

There was no sign of anything like a dust storm in sight. I suppose it was a prophetic premonition of what was about to come. We rushed quickly to get on the plane after leaving the pyramids. As soon as our plane took off, a dust storm erupted out of nowhere. My team remembered that I had just blurted out this statement. I looked out the window, and everywhere was completely white. I could not see a thing. I would soon come to find out that this was a massive dust storm, so massive that the area had not seen one like it in a number of years.

The pilots came on, speaking in a foreign language to alert the passengers. I did not know what they were saying, but I was sure that it was not good. I kept waiting to hear more, but the pilots would not speak in English. The gift of interpretation quickly stirred up in me, to my surprise, and I then could understand them. I told my team, "They're saying that because of the dust storm, they can't see to land the plane."

At that moment, God said to me, *Intercede now. They are not to land here, because if they do the plane will crash.*

I related what God had said to my team, and we immediately began praying in the Spirit loudly. I thought, *It doesn't matter; everyone is foreign on this plane, and they will think we're speaking another language.* Finally, the pilot came on and got out a few words in English. He confirmed what the Holy Spirit had allowed me to hear. The pilot stated that they could not see to land the plane and that they were flying blind. I found out midflight that this plane did not have the technology to deal with such conditions.

Suddenly, the plane took a nosedive! I looked at my team, sitting directly beside me, and told them again, "The Lord said if the pilots try to land here, the plane will crash. He said we must pray that they are diverted!"

The plane leveled out for just a minute, and then it went down again, and then pulled up abruptly. We were still in the thick of a huge dust cloud . . . you could not see a thing outside. This happened at least five or six times—one nosedive after another. The more the pilots would nosedive, the harder and louder we would pray. Finally, they came on and announced that they were diverting the plane and would make an emergency landing elsewhere.

By this time, it was late at night. When we finally made it to the ground, everybody on the plane was shaken up and was anxious to get off. I was sitting there waiting and telling the Lord, *I can't go back up in the air right now. That was a bit too much! I don't know where I am, but I'm not getting on another plane right now!*

Just at that time, an airport worker came on board the plane and asked, "Are there any Americans on this flight?"

My team and I jumped up and rushed to the door to exit. They put us and a few others on an airport tram and took us to the front of what was a very small airport. We asked, "Where do we go from here?"

One worker looked at us and said, "You're on your own."

"What?!" I exclaimed. "Whom do I complain to about this?" I asked.

"The airport is closed now," the worker answered, "but you can talk to someone in the morning."

I quickly found a random taxi van and told the driver, "My team and I just want to get to Israel, but we don't even know where we are."

No one had told us our location since we had landed, by the way. The driver agreed to take us where we needed to be by car. We drove between four and six hours through the night, and finally we arrived at my host's place in Israel.

My host asked us, "Do you know what just happened? Do you know where you just came from?" I answered no, and he informed us, "You took the exact route that the children of Israel took out of Egypt. The plane dropped you off at the Red Sea."

It was at that moment that the Lord allowed me to know that all the agitation and disruption we had just been through was in preparation for the assignment ahead of us in Israel. He downloaded in my spirit that we were in the midst of a shaking because a shaking was coming to Israel. My team and I had to walk through it in the natural as a prophetic demonstration of what I was to announce at the prophetic meetings I was about to be part of in Israel in the days just ahead.

## The Shaking Is from God

A shaking is a violent disruption of a pattern, flow or cycle. When something or someone is shaken, it is an agitation of the current state or condition. Because the old state or condition is being disrupted, after the shaking the condition of the object or entity being shaken will be different. When God brings a shaking, it often comes with what is perceived as destruction. The Lord will send a wind to tear down the old, that which is perverse and those things that are a hinderance to His will. Even in this process, God always has something that will remain, and a new thing will emerge.

The writer's words in Hebrews 12:25–27 give clarity to the process of a shaking that comes from God:

> See that you do not refuse Him who speaks. For if they did not escape who refused Him who spoke on earth, much more shall we not escape if we turn away from Him who speaks from heaven, whose voice then shook the earth; but now He has promised, saying, "Yet once more I shake not only the earth, but also heaven." Now this, "Yet once more," indicates the removal of those things that are being shaken, as of things that are made, that the things which cannot be shaken may remain.

This passage sheds light on what a divine shaking looks like. Currently, as I write this, the world is in a Hebrews 12:25–27 moment. We are seeing this shaking in the earth, and it will continue over the next several years. It is important to note that in this passage of Scripture, God says that He is shaking the earth and heaven. I will revisit this further in a moment, but also notice that this Scripture highlights that God's *voice* shook the earth. That paints a powerful picture and is another indication of what is happening right now.

Prophets are God's ambassadors and mouthpieces in the earth. Seasoned and mature prophets often have the authority and rank to speak *as God's voice* in the earth, not just *for God*. God's prophets and prophetic people are His voice to humanity. He sends the prophets to proclaim and declare

47

His words. These words are ushering in the shaking. The word *voice* in this passage we just read is transliterated as *phōnē* in the Greek, which means "a sound, a tone, a voice, speech."[1] It is the enemy's intent to disconnect people from the *phōnē* through which they hear God. There is a remnant rising up, however, who are connected to God's heart and who carry His voice that will shake the earth, the nations and the heavens.

Let's look at our modern English word *phone*, which comes from the Greek word for *voice* that we just looked at. In our present day, we have watched the phone's progression. We went from landline telephones, to cordless phones, to cell phones, to smartphones. This is the beauty of technology. *Technology* comes from a Greek word meaning "a systems upgrade." As it is in the natural, so it is in the Spirit. When God wants to give us a clearer sound or transmit a clearer signal, He releases Kingdom technology, or a systems upgrade. Think about how phones in the 1980s were somewhat limited to your house, but now with smartphones we can talk on the phone anywhere. I have been to some of the most remote places on the earth, traveling and preaching the Gospel, and people had smartphones and could still get signals. This is symbolic and prophetic. The voice of the Lord is invading every sector of the earth, and God is causing people who are in hidden places to pick up heaven's signal.

I have been prophesying for some time that we are in the midst of a major shaking. Sometimes these words can become cliché to some who have been in the Church for a long time. Many people repeat or echo them without understanding them. Let's explore the word *shake* or *shaken* in the original biblical writings. There are several layers to the definition of these terms. In our Hebrews 12 passage, the word *shaken* is *saleuō* in the Greek. The first part of its definition is "a motion produced by winds, storms, and waves." It further means "to agitate and shake thoroughly." This means that when God is bringing His shaking in the earth, it can often manifest in the natural through violent winds, storms and waves. So His shaking can be both literal and symbolic.

The next part of its definition is "to overthrow, to cast down from one's secure state, to move, to agitate the mind." This deals with removing people, nations or entities from seats of authority and power. It can also deal with changing someone's mental perception and view of a person, place or thing.

## Five Major Areas the Lord Shakes

God's shaking can affect us in many different ways, but you and I must remember that there is a plan and purpose in the shaking. It may seem destructive or violent at first, but God is interested in birthing forth His agenda by removing what needs to be removed. Scripture identifies five major areas that the Lord shakes: (1) *He shakes the earth*, (2) *He shakes the heavens*, (3) *He shakes people*, (4) *He shakes governments*, and (5) *He shakes industries and systems*. Let's explore each of these in greater detail.

### 1. God is shaking the earth.

The earth has been literally groaning in birth pangs, awaiting the manifestation of the sons of God, according to Romans 8:22–24. (Sons in this context does not refer to gender, but rather to position.) I believe that some of the earthquakes and natural disasters that we see now and will see are a sign of the earth being in travail. The earth is directly connected to humanity. The Bible says in Genesis that Adam was made from the dust of the earth (see Genesis 2:7), and after that humans were called sons of Adam. Prophetically, this means that the physical movements we see happening within the earth are symbolic of what God is doing in humanity. This is why the earth is shaking and in travail, because it can sense the time drawing closer. It is yearning for the sons (and daughters) of God to take their positions.

Sometimes when a shaking comes to the earth, it manifests as a famine where food is scarce and the earth is not producing. The first famine the Bible mentions is found in Genesis 12:10. This famine was so fierce that it caused Abraham to make a geographical move to Philistine land within Egypt. Then in Genesis 26:1, Scripture mentions another famine during the time of Isaac. This famine caused Isaac to move to Gerar, where he planted crops in the midst of the famine and became very wealthy. The most notable biblical famine, however, is found in Genesis chapters 41–47. This famine arose in Egypt during the time of Joseph. God transitioned Joseph to Egypt through harsh circumstances beforehand so he could be in position to interpret Pharaoh's dream and prepare in advance to save the Egyptians and all of the children of Israel.

Do you notice the pattern and similarities that surround famines in the Bible? Anytime the earth experienced a famine, God was instituting *transition*—a repositioning and advancement of His agenda. I believe that the Lord still uses famine to bring transition, to reposition and to usher in a new plan. Famine can be spiritual or natural or both, but it is all part of God's shaking.

### 2. God is shaking the heavens.

The Bible speaks of three heavenly domains—the first, the second and the third heaven. Paul says in 2 Corinthians 12:2, "I know a man in Christ who fourteen years ago—whether in the body I do not know, or whether out of the body I do not know, God knows—such a one was caught up to the third heaven. . . ." Here, Paul gives us a clue into the mysteries of the heavens. The early Church believed that there were multiple heavens. The third heaven is where God's abode is, the seat of His throne and domain. The second heaven is what may be referred to as outer space. This is where the celestial bodies (planets and stars) reside, as do spiritual thrones, dominions, principalities and powers. Last, there is the first heaven, which is the sky that we see above us.

The word *heaven* in the Greek is *ouranos*—meaning "the vaulted expanse of the sky with all things visible in it"—the universe, the world and the heavens. It also means "the seat of order of things eternal." So when God shakes the heavens, He is shaking visible and invisible seats of power. According to Colossians 1:16, God originally created and set up spiritual entities to govern and keep the universe in heavenly order. Due to Lucifer's iniquity and his subsequent expulsion from heaven, however, a third of the angels or spiritual beings left with him because he deceived them. This brought corruption within the spiritual ranks, which ultimately corrupted the earth. These spiritual entities are the thrones, dominions, principalities and powers that now reside in the second heaven.

Thrones are governing forces that have spiritual jurisdiction and rule over large portions of the earthly and heavenly territories. Dominions are spiritual entities that govern underneath the rank of thrones, which rule with supreme authority. Then there are principalities, which govern municipalities and cities. When God shakes the heavens, He is therefore shaking the forces of darkness that are in high places. We are in a season where God is exposing wickedness in high and heavenly places and bringing them down.

### 3. God is shaking people.

The Lord is bringing a divine shaking to His people, as well as to humanity as a whole. Within every sector of the world, every industry and every sphere of influence, God is releasing a shift. What people have sown in previous seasons, they are now reaping. The year 2020 ushered us into a decade of reaping in the kingdom of men. This entire decade will be filled with shifting. If a person has sown well, then he or she will reap good things. If a person has sown corruption, however, then he or she will reap corruption.

Based on people's actions, we are seeing shakings result in three types of manifestations: demotions, divine removals and divine promotions. The shakings will cause some people to be demoted—those who have compromised their integrity and have not lived according to the principles of God's Word. They have gone through life's tests and have continued to fail. They will experience a demotion from their places of authority, influence and power. Some of these people may even have been at the top of their industries. Nevertheless, they have been found wanting in the balance, and the Lord will cause them to be greatly humbled.

Further, for some the shaking will result in divine removals. God is removing even some kings or high-ranking leaders from their governmental positions. This will be the release of God's judgment among humankind. Throughout the next ten years, we will continue to see divine judgment resulting in the complete removal of some who have had wicked hearts toward others. The fire of the Holy Spirit is being sent to consume wickedness, arrogance and pride.

As we witness this divinely orchestrated removal of people who have wicked hearts, simultaneously we will see the Holy Spirit coming upon other people who have been proven, tried and tested to replace them. The third shaking will bring about godly promotions. According to Merriam-Webster, *promotion* is "the act or fact of being raised in position or rank; the act of furthering the growth or development of something [or someone]."[2] This is a season of advancement for those who are willing to submit fully to God and to obey His instructions. Just as Samuel anointed David and the Spirit of God was with David afterward, we will see this same experience happen to many. God has a remnant made up of those who have been on the back side of the desert, serving Him faithfully and waiting for the timing of the Lord. Promotion is coming for the remnant . . . the faithful. This will be a promotion in rank, authority, influence, resources and advanced operation in the things of the Spirit.

### 4. God is shaking governments.

We are in a period where nations are hanging in the balance. There is a major war in the heavenlies over the nations. Over the next ten years, we will see multiple shakings hit the nations of the world. There is a reordering of nations unveiling right now, as I write these words. Nations that have ranked at the top among other nations will fall. Other nations will rise due to the remnant of praying believers, innovators and thinkers.

The Lord showed me some developing nations in Africa and other areas that are going to experience complete overhauls in their government infrastructure. These developing countries have been oppressed and kept under strict demonic control. The people living in them have been punished severely due to oppressive regimes, but the Holy Spirit says to me that change is coming. In the days to come, you will see these nations begin to rise out of the ashes, and they will surge forward.

### 5. *God is shaking industries and systems.*

As I was preparing for our annual New Year's Eve service that would take place on December 31, 2019, the Lord spoke to me concerning the world's systems, as He had on many other occasions. This time it was quite odd, because typically our New Year's Eve service is celebratory and upbeat. However, this time was different. I went into prayer in the days leading up to the event, and what the Holy Spirit shared with me shook me to my core. For the few prior years, the Lord had spoken to me about the collapse we would see beginning in 2020 throughout the world. I shared this with my church, but many people did not believe it. At this particular service on the last night of 2019, I prophesied that businesses and conglomerates would be shaken and many would close down. I saw America's sector of wealth hit severely. Then the Lord told me to prepare people for the shaking that would result in a global financial crisis. Some industries will never be the same. Every major world system is going through a recalibration, reconstruction and overhaul. The end result will be a drastic change in the way that life is conducted.

 ## YOUR PROPHETIC FORECAST

Everything that can be shaken, will be shaken. Yes, the world is going through a massive shaking in our day, but so are you individually. A shaking can feel as if your entire world is turned upside down. A shaking can be uncomfortable, to say the least, but it is necessary. A God-ordained shaking season has many benefits. Here are several key points for you to remember as you endure the shaking:

- The shaking is coming with greater glory. You will see the glory (goodness) of the Lord break forth as the sunlight breaks through the early morning darkness. It will bring transformation to your character and will yield much fruit.

- You must allow the Holy Spirit to adjust areas of your life in order for you to move into another dimension of His presence.

- In your personal life, the shaking will uncover wrong relationships, ungodly alliances and unequal partnerships. This period of detachment from these people may cause you to feel emotional pain and aloneness, but God will use it for His purpose.

- God never shakes what He does not intend to process and grow. The shaking will bring dynamic and accelerated growth in your life.

## PROPHETIC HOPE

After the shaking comes the glory. There is beauty that comes from intense seasons of your life. What remains after the shaking is the real blessing. God never prunes without an end result of increase and harvest. After your shaking season, you will come forth with a beautiful testimony, a powerful anointing and a greater weight of the presence of God. Many people can only see the discomfort of the shaking, but fail to see the strategic purpose of God. I decree that you will receive lessons from the shaking and will see God's amazing power manifest in your life.

4

# Issachar Arise

Of the sons of Issachar who had understanding of the times, to know what Israel ought to do, their chiefs were two hundred; and all their brethren were at their command.

1 Chronicles 12:32

According to the Bible, Jacob had thirteen children. His sons became the founders of the tribes that would make up the nation of Israel. Issachar is strategically placed as the ninth son of his father, Jacob, but the fifth child of his mother, Leah. The number nine signifies completeness, birthing and fulfillment. In Scripture, it is connected to prayer and intercession (see Acts 3:1). Five is the number of grace and favor.

Genesis 46:13 mentions that Issachar grew up to have four sons. Tola was the eldest son of Issachar and was head of the Tolaite clan, according to Numbers 26:23. The name Tola was also later given to another descendant of Issachar who would judge Israel for 23 years (see Judges 10:1–2). Tola was a powerful name in the tribe of Issachar, which is why it would be recycled in their genealogy. Tola is akin to the Hebrew word *tola'at*, meaning "worm."[1] This meaning is symbolic of the function of Issachar's sons. Just as a worm has no limbs and can only rely on its mouth, so the members of Issachar's tribe must only rely on the prophetic utterance of God from their mouths.

Tola therefore represents the mouth of God. Issachar is a tribe given to speak the mysteries of God to those who will hear. It is the mouth of God that gives wisdom. It is the mouth of God that warns. It is the mouth of God that gives direction for the future. A tribe of people is being raised up in this hour we live in, too, who will carry the mouth of God. They are the modern-day tribe of Issachar. In the coming days, you will see true prophetic ministry that is Christ centered, with a heavy emphasis on stewarding and releasing the mysteries of God. This tribe of Issachar has the answer in their mouths for the problems that the world is facing.

Those who carry this Issachar anointing will release details in prophecy, visions and dreams of the future that only the Spirit of God could have revealed. Prophecy will become so detailed that men, women and even children who carry this prophetic anointing will have such accuracy that it will seem scary and uncanny to some. Visions will play out as if you are watching a movie. And the Lord will speak forth His word to draw people, that they might believe on Him.

The second son of Issachar was Puah, or in other places Puvah. Little is known about Puah, but we can gain some insight from his name. In Hebrew, his name means "to blast (like a trumpet) or to scream."[2] This denotes force and power coming from the mouth. This name is symbolic of the tribe of Issachar having authority, power and force with their words. Likewise, prophetic people today will arise with greater authority and force. God will place power on your words as you prophesy. As you speak in alignment with God's will, your words will be fulfilled.

Further, Puah spelled slightly differently was also the name of a midwife spoken of in Exodus 1:15. It was she, along with another midwife named Shiphrah, who disobeyed Pharaoh's command to kill all the male Israelite children. The Bible says that these midwives feared God and did not do what Pharaoh instructed. In rabbinical teaching and Jewish tradition, the name Puah can be interpreted as one who uses words to soothe a crying baby.[3] Both spiritually and naturally, Puah is a defender of those who cannot defend themselves.

Puah's name, being associated with Issachar, therefore reveals that the Issachar anointing stops decrees of death and demonic spirits that seek to kill and abort God-given assignments. We have entered into a period of time where there are evil forces desiring to release death and premature death. As the children of God, we will combat that demonic plot with the grace, power and the anointing of Issachar. It is time for Issachar to arise. It is time for those who are called to carry this mantle to stand up in the boldness and power of God.

The third son of Issachar was named Job. Job comes from the Hebrew root word *yabab*, meaning "to bawl" or "to cry out." This brings to light that a large part of the Issachar mantle is intercession—praying, lamenting and standing in the gap for other people. Intercession is a sacred, spiritual act, and it is an expression of the Holy Spirit. Romans 8:26 reveals that the Spirit makes intercession for us with groanings that cannot be uttered or put into words. The word *groan* in this text is a Greek word that denotes an inaudible sigh, grief, prayer or a deep moan. It is a sound of desperation, weeping and passionate prayer.

The sons of Issachar, therefore, carry the sound of prayer. They stand in the gap for those who cannot fight for themselves. Another aspect of Job's name is to cry aloud. This is symbolic of revealing what the Spirit of God is saying, without reservation and with little concern over whether or not it will be received. Those who are used by God to prophesy must do so with grace and love; however, there must also be a holy boldness. Prophets and prophetic people "cry out" the words of the Lord to call people into a deeper place of repentance.

The fourth son of Issachar was Shimron. According to the root word for Shimron in Hebrew, his name means "guardianship." To have guardianship is to be placed in a position where one has the legal responsibility to care for those who cannot care for themselves. Spiritually, this represents a gatekeeper—one who stands in a governing position in the Spirit. A gatekeeper manages the affairs, resources and people in his or her care. To govern the gate is a component of the Issachar anointing. The sons of Issachar therefore carry the responsibility to show care, mercy and love to others, and to lead them spiritually.

By studying the attributes of each of Issachar's direct descendants, we can see the anointing, mantle and function that was placed upon the tribe or sons of Issachar. That same anointing is present in our modern day, and it rests on those who carry a prophetic grace.

## Understanding the Times and Seasons

The Bible states in 1 Chronicles 12:32 that the sons of Issachar "had understanding of the times, to know what Israel ought to do." Spiritual times and seasons shift with the wind, and it is given to us as followers of Christ to know the

mysteries of the times in which we live. In order to understand the times and seasons, we have to go on a journey back
to Genesis—yes, back to Eden, where God first instituted
time.

Two spheres of time operate and coexist in the world in
which we live. There is *chronos* time, which is chronological
and is based on the daily calendar. Then there is *kairos* time,
which is divinely appointed and is based on the spiritual
seasons. (I will talk more about the distinctions between
these two spheres just ahead.) The Bible makes it clear that
time is an important factor in the earthen realm, and time
will always remain while the earth exists (see Genesis 8:22).
As we explore this subject in more detail, you will see that
God has given people the power to choose which sphere of
time they wish to operate in.

In Genesis 2, God formed Adam and placed him in a garden that He planted eastward in Eden. So much mystery
surrounding Eden is now being brought to light for those
who are willing to look deeper into the text. Eden was not
just a garden with flowers and plants and all kinds of beautiful animals. The spiritual significance of Eden is revealed in
the name itself. The Hebrew word *Eden* means "pleasure,
luxury and delight." The Hebrew word for garden is *gan*,
and one of the meanings is "enclosure." The definition of
an enclosure is an area or region that is sealed off. Eden was
therefore not just a physical place of pleasure but was also
a spiritual place of pleasure.

The systems of time and space were vastly different in
Eden than they are today. Time was not limiting to humanity, and things did not decay as they aged. Eden had seasons,
days and years, which were signs or distinguishing marks (see
Genesis 1:14), but the seasons were not harsh and unbear-
able. There was no need to work hard for a harvest because

everything produced naturally. There was no need for rain because the earth watered itself. Everything functioned automatically in the way God had created it to function. In the beginning, time was initiated to govern human productivity, but time did not involve labor, and it served the purpose of humankind.

God told Adam that there was one thing he must never do in the Garden of Eden, and that was to eat of the tree of the knowledge of good and evil (see Genesis 2:17). God informed Adam that the day he ate of it, he would surely die. The word *die* in Hebrew is the word *muwth*. There are several definitions of this word, such as "to be put to death," "be executed," and "die prematurely." All of them may apply in Adam's situation. One definition, however, stands out more than all the others: "to dispatch." This definition speaks volumes regarding the massive changes that took place when Adam and Eve ate of the tree of the knowledge of good and evil. In the Hebrew sense, *dispatch* means to send off to a destination. I believe that when Adam and Eve ate of the forbidden tree, they were sent to another destination in time. Another sphere of time presented itself that was the exact opposite of what they knew. The ground was now cursed with thorns and thistles. The earth no longer yielded a harvest automatically. The ground had to be tilled with great effort and labor. The seasons became very different, presenting harsh winters and extremely hot summers. Time had been shifted. With this alteration, humankind was now forced to live under time's governing force, whereas initially time had served humanity.

From the time that Adam and Eve sinned in the Garden, the people and the nations to come would be relegated to living based on the timetable of the world rather than the timetable that God originally created. Let's fast-forward thousands of years into the future, to the Israelites' captivity at the hands of the Egyptians (see Exodus 1:10–11). Egypt represented the center of the world at that time when it came to the economy, culture and even technology. Egypt was a trendsetter that sent waves of influence throughout the world. Egypt served many gods, however, often seen in graven images and statues, and did not serve the God of Israel. The nation lived according to the timetable of this world. According to biblical history, the Egyptians worshiped the sun and relied on it as their god. Supposedly, this god would give them power and supernatural abilities. The Egyptians were able to do much, or so they thought, with the false powers that the sun provided them.

The Egyptians were so enthralled with the sun that they set their whole calendar system around it. This is known as the solar calendar, and it continues to govern most of the world even to this day. Egyptian culture during the Old Testament displayed how greatly this nation focused on the sun. The sun god's name was Ra, and the sun was a major part of Egyptian symbols and hieroglyphics. The Egyptian people believed the myth that the first king of Egypt had created Ra, and they believed that the pharaohs afterward were Ra's successors. The Egyptians were taught that their pharaohs were gods who came from the sun. They exalted the sun above all else.

The true and living God, the God of Israel, detested the practice of Ra worship. Although the sun is one of God's great creations, He never meant for His people (or anyone) to worship it or come under its rule. When God brought the children of Israel out of their bondage to the Egyptians, He did not just bring them out from under their hard taskmasters. He also brought them out from under their taskmasters' concept of time—the same warped sphere of time that Adam and Eve had created when they had broken God's law.

### *Chronos* Time versus *Kairos* Time

Exodus 12:1–2 (KJV) says, "And the Lord spake unto Moses and Aaron in the land of Egypt saying, this month shall be unto you the beginning of months: it shall be the first month of the year to you." In this passage of Scripture, God speaks to Moses and Aaron concerning the changing of the times. He instructs them that there will be a new time that they will operate in. Because the Egyptians had been so entrenched in their sun worship and a solar calendar, God completely changed this system for the Israelites. He told them that "this month shall be unto you the beginning of months." The word *month* in the Hebrew is the word *chodesh*, and it means "new moon." God gave Moses instructions to sanctify the new moon. Psalm 104:19 (KJV) says that God "appointed the moon for seasons." For the Israelites, this represented the changing of times, but also the changing of seasons.

To further understand the concept of the new moon, we must understand a lunar cycle. In a lunar orbit based on the moon's phases, it takes 29.5 days for the moon to orbit the earth. During this time, the moon changes its appearance several times. It goes from not being seen visibly or illuminated (new moon), to being partially illuminated (waxing crescent), to being fully seen (full moon), then back to being partially illuminated (waning crescent). Then it repeats the cycle, starting with not being illuminated again, which is again known as a new moon.

This whole process takes between 29 and 30 days, which is the amount of time in a month on the Hebrew calendar. The Jewish months are so powerful because each one possesses meaning even within the name of the month itself. This is God's original timetable, and He created the months so that they might prophesy of what is to take place within each month. Each has a specific name and meaning that speaks to what that month will entail and to the key blessings released within it. By locating where these months fall within our modern Gregorian calendar, we can rediscover the mysteries of God as they relate to our modern time.

The sun and the moon represent the two spheres of time that coexist on the earth. These spheres are total opposites, just like night and day. One sphere governs those people who are of the world, while the other sphere directs the children of God. The timetable of the world is *chronos*, or chronological time, but God's time is *kairos*, or divinely appointed time.

As I talked about with Egypt and its sun god, worldly time in Scripture is depicted by the sun. King Solomon understood that there are two spheres of time, and here is what he had to say concerning the sun (with my emphasis added on *under the sun*):

"What profit has a man from all his labor in which he toils *under the sun?*" (Ecclesiastes 1:3).

"That which has been is what will be, that which is done is what will be done, and there is nothing new *under the sun*" (Ecclesiastes 1:9).

"I have seen all the works that are done *under the sun*; and indeed, all is vanity and grasping for the wind" (Ecclesiastes 1:14).

"Then I looked on all the works that my hands had done and on the labor in which I had toiled; and indeed all was vanity and grasping for the wind. There was no profit *under the sun*" (Ecclesiastes 2:11).

"Therefore I hated life because the work that was done *under the sun* was distressing to me, for all is vanity and grasping for the wind" (Ecclesiastes 2:17).

"Then I hated all my labor in which I had toiled *under the sun*, because I must leave it to the man who will come after me" (Ecclesiastes 2:18).

"And who knows whether he will be wise or a fool? Yet he will rule over all my labor in which I toiled and in which I have shown myself wise *under the sun*. This also is vanity" (Ecclesiastes 2:19).

"Therefore I turned my heart and despaired of all the labor in which I had toiled *under the sun*" (Ecclesiastes 2:20).

"For what has man for all his labor, and for the striving of his heart with which he has toiled *under the sun*?" (Ecclesiastes 2:22).

"Moreover I saw u*nder the sun*:
    In the place of judgment, wickedness was there; and in the place of righteousness, iniquity was there" (Ecclesiastes 3:16).

King Solomon released such poignant information concerning life under the sun. He was speaking concerning the system of time that governs this world. Within Ecclesiastes, he reveals the side effects of living under the sun. The first downside is working but having *no* profit. The word *profit* in Hebrew is *yithrown*, meaning "advantage, profit and excellency." To be profitable is to be successful in finance, but also in life. Solomon saw that under the sun's system, there is no productivity. Operating under the sun's system of time brings vexation of spirit. Vexation is the state of being annoyed, frustrated and worried.

If you are constantly experiencing frustration with life, it could be a sign that you are operating under the wrong system of time. All it takes is a simple shift in paradigm to bring you under the right time zone. There is despair under the sun. Despair is the loss or absence of hope. And faith and hope go together (see 1 Peter 1:21). Without faith it is impossible to please God. Faith is the ability to agree with and come into alignment with God's decisions concerning your life, even if you don't understand them.

## God's Timetable

As I said, these two spheres of time, one based on the moon and the other on the sun, coexist and operate like night and day. After all of the writings Solomon released concerning the vanities of operating in a time zone "under the sun," he gave the antidote with which to combat this purposeless system. In Ecclesiastes 3:1 he says, "To everything there is a season, a time for every purpose under heaven." Here, Solomon in all his wisdom reveals that there is only purpose when operating *under heaven*! Heaven is the Hebrew word *Shamayim*, which means "the abode of God." The abode of God is His dwelling place or residence. To be under heaven (the abode of God) is to be submitted to, in agreement with and faithful to God's will.

You must understand that God's will is His time. The will of the Lord is not just a set of instructions or a way to live; it is literally a *system of time*. Time is the Hebrew word *'eth*, which means "experiences, fortunes and occasions." The system of time you submit to will determine what type of experiences, fortunes and occasions you have in your life. The Bible says, "He has made everything beautiful *in its time*. Also, He has put eternity in their hearts, except that no one can find out the work that God does from beginning to end" (Ecclesiastes 3:11, emphasis added).

The whole plan of the enemy from the beginning, going all the way back to the Garden of Eden, was to change the times. And his plan has not changed, even until now. Daniel 7:25 says of him, "He shall speak pompous words against the Most High, shall persecute the saints of the Most High, and shall intend to *change times and law*. Then the saints shall be given into his hand for a time and times and half a time" (emphasis added). The word *change* here means "to alter, transform or frustrate." The enemy literally seeks to alter, transform and frustrate your purpose in order to negatively impact your time.

Nonetheless, with proper information, tools and anointed instructions, you can submit to the right system of time, and God can reset your spiritual calendar to the way it was originally supposed to be! The Issachar anointing gives you the ability to reset your time to God's original plan and purpose for your life. When you have a heart to fully surrender to God's will, He will align you with heaven's timetable and agenda.

## Vision of an Emerging Darkness

The times and seasons are changing so rapidly. We are even seeing the merging and colliding of seasons. We have entered into a decade and an era of the unusual. This time period will be marked by upheaval, and at moments by chaos. In my time of prayer, I saw a vision open up to me of a dark, demonic spirit rising over certain countries and cities. The Holy Spirit said to me that this spirit of darkness has been unleashed because of the time that the world is in. This is the spirit that the Bible calls Abaddon or Apollyon in Revelation 9:11. In the original tongue, this name means "destroyer" or "destroying angel." This spirit's assignment is to ravage and destroy families, churches and individuals called by God. This spirit of darkness has the intention of increasing gun violence, mass murders and senseless killings. The only way to withstand this demonic force is to be anchored in Jesus Christ. Your faith and belief system must be rooted in Him.

## A Breed of Unusual Issachar Prophets

The Lord is mantling a new breed of Issachar prophets. This company of prophets will be different. They will not be concerned with platforms, fame or politics. They will walk heavily in the fear of the Lord. This company will not be caught up in the sins of compromise or competition. They will not be given to chasing money or material possessions. Their emphasis won't be on their skill or talent. They will stand firmly on godly character.

When the prophets in this unusual new breed speak, they will release the words of the Lord with boldness, courage and the fire of God. Some of the words they speak and some of their actions will be very controversial, but the Lord is saying to me, *I will be with them.*

The Issachar prophets are arising to know the times and seasons and to help usher in the next move of the Spirit. They will not fit into the religious box of today. They will not fit into human traditions or play by the rules of the religious sects. They will stand firmly on the Word of God and live righteously. When they speak, revelation knowledge will be revealed.

 **YOUR PROPHETIC FORECAST**

You may be one of the Issachar prophets or one of the prophetic people the Lord is empowering in this hour. I want to affirm that you are so needed for the time that we are in. In the midst of chaos and calamity, you will rise as a voice of clarity, peace and direction for others.

I have learned over the years, however, that many prophetic people have been rejected in the Church not just outside the four walls, but inside. One of the greatest hindrances to an Issachar prophet is developing a wounded and rejected heart. Many times, the enemy uses rejection to attempt to stifle the purpose of a believer. This will not be your portion, because heaven is affirming you right now. God is releasing you from the rejection, fear and painful wounds of the past, in Jesus' name!

To help you better understand the role of an Issachar prophet or a prophetic person, I will list here seven earmarks of the Issachar anointing.

### Seven Earmarks of the Issachar Anointing

1. The Issachar anointing generates abundance and wealth, and gives you access to heaven's economy. This is found in the name *Issachar*. In Hebrew it means "reward, compensation or to repay."
2. The Issachar anointing unlocks a dimension of God's divine timing. Speaking of God's appointed seasons

and moments, 1 Chronicles 12:32 reveals that the sons of Issachar understood the times.

3. The Issachar anointing gives you the ability to lead. The sons of Issachar led the millions of Israelites into the direction that God was taking Israel.

4. The Issachar anointing gives you prophetic insight to identify future kings and prominent leaders. It was the tribe of Issachar that was in favor of David being king and that helped propel him into rulership.

5. The Issachar anointing gives acuity to your spiritual eyesight so that you can know what God is doing in the earth.

6. The Issachar anointing enables those who carry it to have supernatural strength to carry burdens. Genesis 49:14 says, "Issachar is a strong donkey, lying down between two burdens." Issachar people carry the burdens of other people, cities and nations.

7. The Issachar anointing raises up valiant warriors: "Now their brethren among all the families of Issachar were mighty men of valor, listed by their genealogies, eighty-seven thousand in all" (1 Chronicles 7:5).

## PROPHETIC HOPE

We all carry the future within us, as we saw in chapter 1. Even if you are not a prophet, the prophetic essence of God dwells within you, and you carry eternity in your heart. If the Lord is mantling you among His new breed of prophets, however, then the Issachar anointing is coming upon you to provide clear direction and instruction from the Lord. You will know how to navigate the times and seasons. And in the days ahead, God is sending you angelic reinforcement to usher you into new spiritual and natural domains. The Issachar anointing will break open the abundance of heaven over you. You will see new doors of opportunity, Kingdom connections and resources. This anointing comes with great boldness. You will boldly declare the plans and purposes of God in the earth, without fear. You will arise as the Issachar anointing is rising in your life.

5

# Nations and Kingdoms

Then the seventh angel sounded: And there were loud voices in heaven, saying, "The kingdoms of this world have become the kingdoms of our Lord and of His Christ, and He shall reign forever and ever!"

Revelation 11:15

Years ago, before fully accepting the call to ministry, I was sitting in a service, intrigued by the prophetic gifts in operation. I was not really operating in the gifts of the Spirit at the time. And this was not the church I attended, so I felt a little out of place because some of the experiences were different. One thing I knew for sure: God was definitely there.

I had always had a leaning toward the supernatural. I would later find out that most prophetic people do. The gifts in a person's life must be guarded, purified and submitted to the Lordship of Jesus Christ. This keeps our gifts from being contaminated, and it helps us not get pulled into the false supernatural or the demonic. At that time, because of my insatiable desire to learn the ways of the Holy Spirit, I was learning whatever I could about the spiritual gifts.

Back to the service—there was a prophet up preaching and calling people out spontaneously to give them what seemed to be accurate words about their lives and their futures. His gift was quite uncanny, based on the reactions of those receiving a word. Other people were worshiping the Lord, and some were on their knees, repenting at the altar. It was one of the most memorable experiences I had before I came into the work of the ministry. I had never seen this speaker before. He had flown in from another state. I was sitting in the middle of the congregation, not too close to the front and not too far from the back. There was an art to where I had positioned myself. I was trying to hide and blend in with the crowd. It didn't work. In the middle of ministering, the prophet turned and called me out: "You, come to the front!"

He startled me a bit. Trembling, I walked to the front with my hands lifted. He began to prophesy to me, and it flowed out of him like water: "The Lord says that you are a prophet to the nations. You will travel throughout the world, ministering the Word of the Lord. This will start for you at a young age. You will travel to South America and Europe and Africa. I see you speaking to large groups of Spanish-speaking people and people who speak other languages." Then he shouted, "God says, '*You are a prophet to the nations, like Jeremiah, and you will go wherever I send you!*'"

I was stunned by the directness of these words of the Lord. They hit my spirit like electricity. Further, this sent me on a quest to understand the phrase *prophet to the nations.* What did that mean? As I began to search for the meaning and dig into the term *nations,* in its simplest form I found it to mean "people groups; ethnicities."[1] On my journey, the Lord was teaching me the value of people and how precious they are to Him. People from every culture, continent and background—He loves people. Sometimes we think *nations* only means places where we land when we are traveling to far lands or obscure places. But *nations* are right there in your backyard and in your neighborhood. In that regard, we are all called to the nations. That's right, you are called to the nations. You are called to connect with and serve all kinds of people.

Psalm 2:8 says, "Ask of Me, and I will give You the nations for Your inheritance, and the ends of the earth for Your possession." The greatest inheritance you can have will be found in Kingdom relationships with other people. Money does not make a person wealthy; it is the currency of relationships in the Body of Christ that keeps us strong.

## The Kingdoms of This World

In modern terms, Jeremiah would be referred to as a governmental prophet. He was the kind of prophet who had an assignment to nations, kings and queens. Jeremiah also had the assignment of warning the people about what was to come in the future. This is one of the functions of modern prophets; they warn God's people of impending danger, judgment or disaster. Prophetic voices are called to reveal God's heart and mind, as well as the mysteries of what lies ahead.

Jeremiah also had the responsibility prophetically to speak of the next phase that would come for the nation. God tells Jeremiah that He has elevated him. Jeremiah was around seventeen years old, but he had an old man's maturity in spiritual years. Natural age is not a determining factor in how God will use you. The most important factors are what the Lord has called an individual to do, the assignment on that person's life, and the mantle that the person carries.

Jeremiah tells the Lord that he cannot do what he is being asked because he is too young, but the Lord admonishes him never to say that he is too young, and tells him that he will go wherever he is sent. This is the lesson: You are never too old or too young to do what God has called you to do.

In Jeremiah 1:10 the Lord says to Jeremiah, "I have this day set you over the nations and over the kingdoms." To fully understand what Jeremiah's elevation entailed, we must look at the original definition for *nations* and *kingdoms* in this verse. *Nations* means a community of people based on a common language, territory, history, and ethnicity. It comes from the Latin word *natio*, which means birth or tribe.[2] So here we see God telling Jeremiah that He is putting him over groups of people. This means that God was releasing the authority for Jeremiah to prophesy to nations, and that the prophet's words would affect groups of people who were of the same tribe, ethnicity and background naturally.

God also tells Jeremiah that He has set him over kingdoms. *Kingdom* here comes from the Greek word *basilia*, which means "realm or rule." More importantly, the root word for kingdom is *foot*. You can see the connection in Joshua 1:3, where God told Joshua, "Every place that the sole of your foot will tread upon I have given you." Wherever the sole of Joshua's foot tread, God gave him that territory. Likewise, because the Kingdom of God is within us, whenever we walk or move, we are transporting the Kingdom of God with us. We are literally carrying God's realm and His rule along with us! The Kingdom of God is within you. It is in your feet. Wherever He sends you, whenever you place your feet upon that ground, it is a prophetic act that you are advancing the Kingdom.

The word *kingdom* has a strong connection to our modern-day word for systems. Kingdoms are spheres, realms and domains of influence, and so are systems within the world. Revelation 11:15 (KJV) states, "And the seventh angel sounded; and there were great voices in heaven, saying, 'The kingdoms of this world are become the kingdoms of our Lord, and of his Christ; and he shall reign for ever and ever.'" According to Scripture, the kingdoms of this world are converted to the kingdoms of our Lord Jesus Christ. This simply means that Christ has rulership over everything. And because we are in Him, we rule with Him. As a believer, when you are aligned with God's agenda in the earth, you can speak the words of the Lord and then the systems within the world must yield to the power of God within you.

Notice that Revelation 11:15 uses the phrase "*kingdoms of this world.*" The word for *world* in Greek is *cosmos*. It means "a beautifully ordered and harmoniously put together and well-arranged system." This means that kingdoms and systems are synonymous. Knowing that kingdoms are tied to systems, we can see that God is telling Jeremiah (Jeremiah 1:10) that He is putting him over nations (groups of people) and kingdoms (systems of the world).

The study of biology often identifies six kingdoms of living things, although some schools of thought identify up to twelve. Whatever their divisions, these kingdoms make up the world as we know it. In this day, God has given believers authority over each one. This extends from the plant kingdom to the animal kingdom to the kingdom of man. Jesus Christ was sent to realign and reconcile the kingdoms and systems of this world back to the Father. John 3:16 (KJV) says, "For God so loved the world, that he gave his only begotten Son, that whosoever believeth in him should not perish, but have everlasting life." This Scripture says that God so loved the *world*, not the earth, which again is the word *cosmos* and includes everything in creation and the universe. In its proper context, this Scripture is conveying that God so loved all of creation that He sent His only begotten Son into the systems of the world. According to John 3:17, the Father did not send His Son into the *cosmos* to condemn the *cosmos*, but to save the *cosmos*. So, God did not just send Jesus into the earth to defend it and to save and redeem people; He sent Jesus into the systems of the world to redeem the systems as well.

How, then, will God redeem the systems? How will He restore the kingdoms of this world? He will use true believers to continue this restorative and redemptive work of the systems and the *cosmos*. The Bible says. "As He is, so are we in this world" (1 John 4:17). We are God's hands and feet in the earth. God is placing His people into every system of the world to advance His agenda. Some believers will be raised up as business leaders, others will be raised up as doctors, some will be raised up as schoolteachers and so forth. God is placing His people everywhere to fulfill His heart and mind in every system.

## YOUR PROPHETIC FORECAST

You are multidimensional, meaning you have a calling and assignment within the Church, and also an assignment to the world. Many believers find it difficult to reconcile the two. Some never quite figure out their place within the Body of believers, but they succeed in being effective in their role in their community. Others are very effective in a church setting, but they are obsolete outside those four walls. As we move forward quickly on God's timetable, a demand is being placed on many believers who have dual responsibilities. You will carry a priestly anointing to the Church and a kingly anointing to the world. The Church needs a priest, but the world needs a king.

God is equipping you to go into both spheres with His grace and accomplish your assignments. By embracing this multilayered mandate, you will become a change agent who will positively disrupt systems and groups of people with a message of love and hope. Here are some takeaways to help you navigate your involvement with nations and kingdoms:

- Your spiritual inheritance is found in people. As I mentioned earlier, Psalm 2:8 informs us that we can ask God, and He will give us nations (people groups) for our legacy.
- God is spiritually sowing you into the world systems to make an impact. You are called to both the Church and the world.
- Wherever the soles of your feet touch, you have an opportunity to advance the Kingdom of God. Never underestimate the power of your feet touching the ground.

## PROPHETIC HOPE

Yahweh (the Lord God) is the God of inheritance. He desires greatly to give you an inheritance. There is treasure being stored up for you in heaven. On this earth, however, you will receive wealth and inheritance through relationships. You will receive souls into the Kingdom of God. The nations and systems of this world have been given over into the hands of God's people. This means that you will take new territory.

6

# Monetary Systems

No one can serve two masters. Either you will hate the one
and love the other, or you will be devoted to the one and
despise the other. You cannot serve both God and money.

Matthew 6:24 NIV

One of the hardest tests I had to endure in ministry, business
and life is one time when the Lord gave me a big vision, but
I did not have the money to fund it. I remember needing to
step out in faith to do a ministry project that would help
thousands of people. I thought to myself, *God, why would
You give me this plan or vision if You know the budget is
fifty times the amount I have in my bank account?*

Over the years, God has had me start various projects,
such as feeding programs for families in need, community
initiatives, sponsoring underprivileged children, and putting
together ecumenical gatherings among many other things.
Each time the Lord spoke to me about doing one of these
projects, I would be so excited to be helping others. Serving

was ingrained in me from a young age, and I love seeing others blessed and empowered by the Word and love of God.

Midway through a particular project, however, my excitement started to diminish as I realized I did not have the money to make it happen. There were venue expenses, people waiting and everything in place, except the money. I had saved and planned and done all the right things in the months leading up to this community endeavor, but something came up outside my control that increased the budget significantly. I was embarrassed, and if I can be honest, a little upset with God. Pride rose up in me as I reminded God of all the things I had done to please Him, and now I thought, *How could this be happening to me?*

You know, God had to be looking at me and thinking, *He has no clue that I am trying to help him.*

I struggled through the project, and I did complete it. Afterward, I was thirty thousand dollars in debt. I told the Lord, *I love You with all my heart, but I will never ever do anything else like that if You ask me again.*

For the next few weeks, I was depressed, but I prayed and still served through it so other people were unaware of my situation. I happened to speak at a small event around that same time. After I finished preaching, a prophet took the mic and said, "The Lord says there is someone here who is in debt. Your account is so negative right now." She emphasized how huge the debt was with her body language.

I thought, *Oh, my gosh, I'm the speaker for this event and God is talking about me. Just sit here and act normal!*

She then said, "But God says the money is going to come from an unexpected place. He says, *You would never think of this place that I will send the money from. But your provision is coming.*"

I was grateful for the word, but I thought, *God really has just read my mail.* Within days after this word, a person whom I had prophesied to years before came to me with a testimony. She was up in age and never had much in terms of natural possessions. She was the last person you would expect to be the conduit of provision. She told me, "The word you gave me came to pass, and the Lord has blessed me."

Not knowing what I needed, she wrote a check for the exact amount of money I still needed to pay off the debt. At that moment, I cried because of God's love and provision. God spoke to me in such a warm, yet stern way, like the amazing Father He is, and said, *See, I don't need your money to complete the things I've called you to do. I am the provision you need, and I have resources everywhere.*

I cried even more and repented before the Lord. I said to Him, *I'm so sorry that I told You I would never do these kinds of projects again. I repent!*

It was through that experience that I forged a new trust with the Lord. It was that day that I learned money is just a construct and God is in control of everything.

## Money Systems Are Changing

There will be a time in the near future where the money system as we know it will be completely changed. Digital currencies will run the world. The U.S. dollar will no longer be the leading currency, and the world's economies will be in travail. But the Lord showed me that before all these things occur, the literal faces on American money will change. This will be a foreshadowing and sign of a steep decline and a swift change that is coming to the economy.

Why would God speak concerning monetary systems? He gives us insight to know what will occur in the future, so that we can mentally and naturally prepare. Money is an overriding force in this natural world. To a degree, it controls where the average people can go, where they can live, what they can drive and what they can eat. Using it is just part of life for us. Money in and of itself is simply a tool given to fulfill certain tasks in life.

Since the beginning of time, there has always been a system of currency. Before we can understand the future of the changing monetary systems, it is important that we understand a little bit about the past and how these systems started. In ancient periods, they used a system of trading and bartering. Some societies have used precious metals like silver or gold. Eventually, this developed into bank notes, or what we now have today as paper money. This entire system has created the more modern platforms of digital currencies like Ethereum and Bitcoin.

A monetary system is defined as institutions, frameworks or a set of policies by which a government creates money within an economy.[1] There are three categories or types of monetary systems: commodity money, commodity-based money and fiat money. Commodity money is made up of precious metals and other commodities that hold their value even when they are melted down, such as gold and silver coins. Then there is commodity-based money, a system where the value of money is based on a commodity but does not involve handling it directly. For instance, the United States used to abide by the gold standard. This meant that the government would convert dollars to gold at a fixed value. In 1933, President Franklin D. Roosevelt took the U.S. off the gold standard. The following year, the government set and held to a $35 per ounce price, until August 15, 1971, when President Richard Nixon announced that America would no longer convert dollars to gold at a fixed value, thereby abandoning the gold standard.[2]

Fiat money is a system of currency by which a government decrees what the legal tender is for its territory. Most monetary systems today involve fiat money because most governments use bank notes or bank balances to back purchases made. This is a system that records credits and debits.

## The War with Mammon

The force ruling the monetary systems of the world is an evil entity called Mammon. Jesus in His earthly ministry revealed that this false god of greed, money and material possessions is attached to a lust for things. As we read at the start of this chapter, He told us in Matthew 6:24 that we cannot serve two masters—we cannot serve God and Mammon. In the original biblical text of this verse, Jesus used the word *mammonas*, a Greek term of Aramaic origin. It literally means "confidence in money." It refers to riches in the sense of their being opposed to the true and living God. Some scholars believe that Mammon was an ancient Syrian or Chaldean (Babylonian) god similar to the Greek god Plutus. Mammon is a demonic spirit or principality that amasses gain through fleshly and worldly means. It is an evil spirit of lust and excess that governs the minds of the people who serve it.

Not all money and riches are from the true and living God. Some is ill-gotten gain or is funding in accordance with a demonic agenda. If a person grows in sin and money at the same time, you can be sure that the riches that individual is receiving are not from God.

The epic battle between light and darkness is a battle between masters. Mammon runs the world systems, from the pharmaceutical industries to the entertainment industries to almost any other industry you can name. Unfortunately, in this world we have seen that people are not valued, but making money is. In the coming days, you will see God bringing a separation between masters. Those who are serving this false god Mammon will bear the corrupt fruit of it. Those who are serving the God of Abraham, Isaac and Jacob will bear the fruit of righteousness.

In 1 Timothy 6:10 we are told that the love of money is the root of all evil. Money in and of itself is not evil; it is the *love* of money that corrodes the soul. A lot of people are chasing money, only to find themselves empty and void. Money cannot fulfill a person. Money cannot heal or restore someone. Money simply takes on the heart of the individual who holds it. Money is an amplifier. It amplifies what is in the soul. If a person is deceitful, add money and his or her deceiving ways will increase. If a person is prideful, add money and he or she will be even more arrogant. Likewise, if a person's heart is pure, money will amplify that pure heart to others. If a person is compassionate, money will provide new avenues through which he or she can give. Money is no more than a tool that amplifies you.

Life is not about those who have and those who don't. Life is not about how much money you have; it is about whom you serve. It is imperative that as a believer in Jesus Christ, you make it crystal clear that you are only serving Him. The time will come in the near future when many people will lose massive amounts of money. I saw in a vision a stock market crash that would shake the nations. There is a time coming where multimillionaires will lose their fortunes in one day. Those who have trusted in wealth will be greatly confounded. Because of the major shaking coming to the earth in this era, even some of the billionaires of our time will be shaken and will be hemorrhaging cash. In this vision from God, I saw very wealthy people selling off their possessions, trying to mitigate their losses due to a massive recession. This will mark a period of a great natural and spiritual famine. (I will talk about this in more detail in the next chapter, "The Days of Joseph Return.") There is a coming famine like the world has never seen, and we must put our trust in God and not in things.

To win the battle against the false god Mammon, you must have a pure and submitted heart before God. You must end your chase for money and began seeking the Lord. After Jesus speaks of Mammon in Matthew 6:24, He goes on to give instructions relating to money and possessions for every believer to follow: "But seek first the kingdom of God and His righteousness, and all these things shall be added to you" (verse 33). Seeking the Kingdom of God is a lifelong assignment as you pursue your purpose in Him. To seek His Kingdom is to seek His rulership. It is to surrender your life to His supreme authority.

Notice how Jesus also says to seek God's righteousness. *Righteousness* in this text is a Greek word meaning "equitable character, justification or to be in right standing with God." We can only seek righteousness by fully submitting ourselves to the Lordship of Jesus Christ. He has to be your Lord, your Master, your Ruler, your everything! At that point only does He say, "and all these things shall be added to you." It is important to remember that you cannot get so wrapped up in the gift that you forget the One who gave it. Everything you need will be attracted to or added to your purpose as you go. If you don't have the money you need, it is because you are not carrying out your assignment. Money is attracted to your assignment.

## Cryptocurrencies and the Stock Market

In the vision from God about monetary systems changing, I saw a deconstruction come to the cryptocurrency market.

85

The period of deconstruction will cause many losses in the markets. Money will be changing hands. This will not just be another dip or decline. God said to me, *It is a deconstruction to bring forth a reconstruction.* Over the next several years, you will see more regulations placed on the markets. But the Lord said to me, *Look to the future, because the markets will expand.*

Cryptocurrencies will become the wave of the future. It will become more and more normal for people to make purchases with its coins. New altcoins and meme coins will arise, and their emergence will baffle those who have their eyes on the markets. The entire crypto system is being overhauled behind the scenes. New prominent players in this space will come to the forefront. The Asian nations will lead in this space. It will take the wisdom of God to navigate these changes in order for one's investments to be unscathed.

The crypto and stock markets will enter into a long and drawn-out period of volatility. God will use this volatility to teach people never to put their trust in mere money or temporal things. Our trust must be only in the Lord Jesus Christ. As this shaking comes to the markets, you will see something new emerge out of the chaos—new monetary systems, platforms and avenues for trading. This will be the reconstruction of the monetary systems that the Lord spoke to me about.

### Prophecy of a Transfer of Wealth

The Spirit of the Lord said to me that there will be a massive wealth transfer to God's Kingdom agents. This will be confounding to many, because during the famine and economic shifts God's remnant will prosper and thrive. According to Haggai 2:8, "'The silver is Mine, and the gold is Mine,' says the LORD of hosts."

This verse connects wealth to an army term, *Lord of Hosts*. Some translations interpret it as the *Lord of the armies of heaven*. Wealth and warfare are often connected. There are angels that release wealth to the people of God, at His word. God controls the nations' economies. The gold is His. The silver is His, and all things in and upon the earth.

As a believer, you will not have to worry about your provision. It will be taken care of. There will be supernatural financial provision coming. God is releasing angels of wealth to facilitate this transfer.

In addition, the Lord is going to deal with wicked people who have oppressed and mistreated others. As the judgment of God is released upon them, their wealth will fall into the hands of the righteous. In the coming months and years, we will see Proverbs 13:22 (ISV) manifest in the earth: "the wealth of the wicked is reserved for the righteous." The next couple of decades will reveal a massive wealth transfer. This will show up in the form of money, land and resources.

## Four Prophetic Winds

We will also see the four winds of the Spirit blowing to release the abundance and supernatural refreshing of God upon His people. Scripture makes several references to the four winds of God. These winds of God bring change, breakthrough, life and even abundance from heaven.

One mention of the four winds is in Ezekiel 37, where God took the prophet Ezekiel into a valley full of dead men's bones. The Bible says the bones were dry, so clearly the bones were from a generation of people who had been dead for many years. There was no sign of flesh on them.

The Lord asked Ezekiel, "Son of man, can these bones live?" and the prophet responded, "O Lord GOD, you know" (verse 3).

Then God gave Ezekiel these instructions: "Prophesy to these bones, and say to them, 'O dry bones, hear the word of the LORD'" (verse 4).

After Ezekiel prophesied and commanded the bones to live, they came together. Next, God gave him instructions to prophesy to the four winds: "Prophesy to the breath, prophesy, son of man, and say to the breath, 'Thus says the Lord GOD: "Come from the four winds, O breath, and breathe on these slain, that they may live"'" (verse 9).

God created these four winds with specific functions. Each wind has a distinct assignment in the earth, and wind or spirit is currency in the spiritual world. The etymology of the word *currency* is something that flows. Wind has a current, and water has a current. The winds of God are modes of transportation that bring things from heaven to earth. By discovering the Hebrew meanings of the four winds, we can better understand their functions:

1. *North Wind*—Hebrew *tsaphan*, meaning "to treasure, store up, treasure up, a quantity of precious gems, metals or other valuables" (see Proverbs 25:23; Song of Solomon 4:16). The north wind releases treasures and resources that have been hidden in darkness. When you are in need of provision and resources, you can prophesy to the north wind.

2. *South Wind*—Hebrew *teyman*, meaning "territory, direction, to choose the right, to use the right hand; denoting power, authority and influence" (see Psalm 78:26). The south wind is a spiritual currency that releases land (both spiritually and naturally),

direction and influence. The south wind releases an anointing for acquisitions and expansion of territory.

3. *East Wind*—Hebrew *qadam*, meaning to meet, come or be in front (see again Psalm 78:26). The east wind brings about a shift in position or rank. It is a wind that brings what was hidden in the back to the forefront. Depending on how it is used, it can signify divine connections, or also disconnection. God uses the east wind to bring the right people into your life and to bring you in front of the right people. This is also a wind of rearranging and reordering. Additionally, God used the east wind as an instrument of judgment; to scatter and to break up.

4. *West Wind*—Hebrew *yam*, meaning "to roar, mighty river, the sea" (see Exodus 10:19). The Bible often uses the sea to represent people, the world, nations or turbulent changes within the nations. Further, the sea can represent a greater depth of knowledge or revelation. The Lord uses the west wind to bring forth resources from people and nations.

## YOUR PROPHETIC FORECAST

As Kingdom citizens, we are in this world, but we are not of this world. Just as business is transacted in the natural, we are called to transact business in the heavens. There are seven levels of currency that you must learn to use wisely. Money is the lowest form. Discovering and properly utilizing each of these currencies will empower you to navigate the purpose of God with ease and with grace.

### Seven Levels of Currency

1. Money—the lowest currency in the earthly realm. It governs business and trade.
2. Communication—the currency of relationships. It helps build covenants, alliances and partnerships.
3. Wisdom—the currency of governments. It creates systems, categories and subcategories to establish order.
4. Influence (favor)—the currency of kings. It is the ability to impact the hearts and minds of others; it is the power of divine persuasion.
5. Faith—the currency of the Kingdom of God. Supporting and defending God's decisions for a person's life through his or her application of the Word, this currency can move mountains.
6. Glory—the currency of heaven. The riches in glory reveal expressions of who God is. There are about a dozen Hebrew words for *glory* that each express a portion of God's goodness. (I will talk about eleven of them in more detail in chapter 20, "Glory Awakening.") Sin causes a person to fall short of this currency.
7. Time—the currency of man. Appointments, dates and divine moments all come under this category of currency. Believers have the authority to redeem (buy back) this currency through salvation. This currency, time, is Satan's downfall because the Bible says that he has a short time and then he will be cast into the lake of fire (see Revelation 12:12; 20:10).

 **PROPHETIC HOPE**

Philippians 4:19 says, "And my God shall supply all your need according to His riches in glory by Christ Jesus." Your provision and supply are only found in the presence of the Lord. He promises in His Word to take care of His children. No matter the economic shifts that occur, you will be firmly positioned under heaven's economy. All your needs will be supplied. This is a prophetic declaration for your life. Receive it, believe it and walk in it!

# 7

# The Days of Joseph Return

> What is happening now has happened before, and what will
> happen in the future has happened before, because God
> makes the same things happen over and over again.
>
> Ecclesiastes 3:15 NLT

The economies of the nations are in transition. As the reordering and rank of the nations continue to change, you will see Western economies tank and some developing nation economies begin to rise. The Lord says, *This decade will be filled with global economic shifts. Money will change hands, and a new monetary system and market will emerge.*

God showed me a vision and spoke to me about the days of Joseph returning. These days are actually here even now, as I write this. God gave Joseph a prophetic interpretation for his time in Genesis 45 that still speaks to us today. The Lord had allowed Joseph to know that the nation of Egypt would come into a period of years where there would be abundance, but immediately following would come a famine like they had never seen. Joseph recognized that God had ordered the events of his life so that he could prepare for what was coming and could help preserve the lives of others, especially his family. Just like what happened in Joseph's time, in a vision the Lord showed me a severe famine and massive shortage coming to the world in our time. A prophecy that is released in the earth realm never dies. Prophecies can be fulfilled, and some can even fail, but if a prophecy is from God, it can never die. I call this a prophetic continuum. It is a series of events that repeats itself at key times in history.

Genesis 41 details a famine so severe that it left many people without food and caused mass death. According to the biblical account, the famine lasted seven years and affected the entire Mediterranean. Archeological and climatological records show that a series of droughts and famines encompassed the civilizations surrounding the Mediterranean at that time in history. The time period of the famine in Joseph's Day is placed at the end of the Bronze Age. This famine even extended beyond Asia Minor and the Mediterranean. One scholarly article comments, "Greece was affected, and the Mycenean culture, with its luxurious palaces, collapsed."[1] Other civilizations in the Italian and Greek islands, including Sicily and Sardinia, were destroyed. People of the Hittite empires were displaced and began to wander. History records these events as being due to an extremely severe series of droughts.

This was no ordinary famine; it lasted for years and caused the collapse of some of the well-known civilizations of its time. History also records that several empires came to Egypt for help. Not only had God given Joseph a wise plan of preservation, but Egypt was also situated on the Nile River.

Egypt was accustomed to depending on the Nile as a source of water rather than on rain, as other areas of the world did.

By virtue of Pharaoh's position and God's master plan, God gave Pharaoh two dreams before any of this occurred. Pharaoh's dreams are recorded in Genesis 41:1–8:

> Then it came to pass, at the end of two full years, that Pharaoh had a dream; and behold, he stood by the river. Suddenly there came up out of the river seven cows, fine looking and fat; and they fed in the meadow. Then behold, seven other cows came up after them out of the river, ugly and gaunt, and stood by the other cows on the bank of the river. And the ugly and gaunt cows ate up the seven fine looking and fat cows. So Pharaoh awoke. He slept and dreamed a second time; and suddenly seven heads of grain came up on one stalk, plump and good. Then behold, seven thin heads, blighted by the east wind, sprang up after them. And the seven thin heads devoured the seven plump and full heads. So Pharaoh awoke, and indeed, it was a dream. Now it came to pass in the morning that his spirit was troubled, and he sent and called for all the magicians of Egypt and all its wise men. And Pharaoh told them his dreams, but there was no one who could interpret them for Pharaoh.

Before this time, Joseph had been chosen by God as a seventeen-year-old boy. Genesis 37:2 calls him a lad. He was favored of his father, who gave him a coat of many colors. One time, Joseph brought to his father an evil report about his brothers. This was at the same time that God had given Joseph a couple of symbolic dreams that one day his family would bow before him. The dreams revealed that one day Joseph would become great among his family and among the nations. Yet it is interesting that at this point Scripture calls him a lad. In Hebrew *lad* is the word *na'ar*, meaning "the age of infancy, a baby or a child." In the Yiddish tongue, it means "fool or foolish." It denotes someone who is emotionally immature.

We see this same word in Jeremiah 1:7, when God called Jeremiah to be a prophet to the nations and told him, "Do not say, 'I am a youth [*na'ar*],' For you shall go to all whom I send you, and whatever I command you, you shall speak." At the time Jeremiah received this word from God he was around the age of seventeen, the same age as Joseph. So the Scripture calls one lad young and foolish, and to the other lad God says, "Do not say you are young and foolish." These two were the same age, but they had different levels of emotional and spiritual maturity. For this reason, Joseph had to go through a series of intense and severe training sessions. God was not being cruel to him; He was taking him through a process where he would build character, maturity and favor.

You have probably heard Joseph's story before. He was thrown into a pit by his own brothers and left for dead. They returned and pulled him out, and then sold him to Ishmaelite slavers for twenty pieces of silver. Afterward, Joseph's brothers lied to their father, Jacob, and told him that Joseph had been killed by an evil beast (see Genesis 37:12–36). Through these horrible events, Joseph's journey of purpose began. He was brought to Egypt, and it was there that an officer of Pharaoh named Potiphar bought him from the Ishmaelites. Genesis 39:2 (KJV) says, "And the LORD was with Joseph, and he was a prosperous man; and he was in the house of his master the Egyptian."

Did you notice the change in Joseph's process? Genesis chapter 37 calls him an emotionally immature boy, while chapter 39 calls him a prosperous man. What caused such a drastic change? In a decade, Joseph had gone through the worst trials of his life. He had been betrayed, left for dead, sold into slavery and eventually falsely accused by Potiphar's wife, which got him thrown into federal prison. All the while, God was maturing, refining and preparing Joseph to stand in position as a father to Pharaoh, a prophet to Egypt and a preserver of Israel.

When no one else could interpret Pharaoh's prophetic dream, Joseph did. He told Pharaoh that there would be seven years of plenty, followed by seven years of severe famine. The famine was so devastating that it erupted in five destructive ways. It is very important that we pay attention to what occurred back then, because we will see it happen again in this new era that we live in. First, *there was no bread*, according to Genesis 47:13. Second, *the money failed*, as stated in verse 15. Third, verse 18 reveals that the people had no livestock, so *they could not work*. Fourth, *they could not hold onto their land and houses*, as mentioned in verse 19. And fifth, the *people were moved into the cities*, says verse 21. A migration occurred due to the famine.

## Prophecy of a Coming Famine

What has happened before, will happen again. I speak this prophetically, that the new era will bring about another severe famine. Among the nations and even in developed countries, food shortages will become the norm. There will be lengthy periods were some meats and other food items will not be available. I saw this vivid vision of the store shelves empty because of a massive food shortage.

In addition, the Lord showed me shortages that would come in other industries such as the pharmaceutical industry. In the vision, I saw common medications that would be hard to find, and their prices would soar. Although we have experienced a shortage of oil in the past, I saw this happening off and on again in the coming years. A time will come when gas is priced so high per gallon that it will greatly impact people's personal budgets. Some people will panic, but the Lord says, *At that time, I will move in miracles of multiplication and supernatural provision for those who believe.*

Further, I saw crop failures coming to the United States and other regions. These failures will be the worst we have seen in more than a fifty-year span. They will happen due in part to the extreme droughts we will see, but also because the earth will be crying out and be in travail. In the vision, I saw that these crop failures will result in a record-breaking more than $49 billion in crop losses.

That day will come, and when it does, intercessors must begin to pray and speak to the rains and command them to water the earth. They must pray that the earth would be replenished and fruitful, for that season of droughts will be one of the worst in history and will greatly impact the agricultural industry. We will also see the cattle industry negatively impacted, as there will be a struggle to keep up with demands. This will give way to a new wave and acceptance of lab-grown meat. This cell-grown meat will begin to take over in the grocery stores en masse.

**Mobilize around the Prophecy**

God has always used His prophets from Old Testament through New Testament times to warn of these kinds of crises. In Acts 11:27–28, a company of prophets journeyed from Jerusalem to Antioch. Christianity was exploding at the time, breaking out of Jerusalem and moving into Gentile nations and the world. Out of the company of prophets arose Agabus, a prophet Scripture only mentions on a few occasions. The Bible says that he predicted by the Spirit that there would be a worldwide famine:

> And in these days prophets came from Jerusalem to Antioch. Then one of them, named Agabus, stood up and showed by the Spirit that there was going to be a great famine throughout all the world, which also happened in the days of Claudius Caesar.

The New Testament prophet Agabus saw the famine coming by the Spirit and mobilized the company of prophets and the Church to be proactive. This is one of the many advantages of the prophetic gift. The Spirit of prophecy points us to Jesus Christ—His heart, character and message. Prophecy gives us the ability to see something before it occurs so that we can align with heaven's agenda concerning that particular situation, occurrence or event. We are given this advantage in order to plan ahead and build around the word that God speaks.

Acts 11:29–30 says this: "Then the disciples, each according to his ability, determined to send relief to the brethren dwelling in Judea. This they also did and sent it to the elders by the hands of Barnabas and Saul." Based on the prophecy, each of the followers of Christ began to act, according to their own abilities and skill sets. This is a brilliant strategy that the New Testament Church put into practice, and we can learn from this example. In a time of famine, scarcity or lack, the Church of Jesus Christ must come together and utilize the talents and skills of each person to send relief to those in need. Families, organizations, churches and communities can pool resources together to survive and thrive in a time of a famine.

The early Church taught us that we are stronger together. Isaiah 65:8 says, "The new wine is found in the cluster, and one says, 'Do not destroy it, for a blessing is in it.'" This verse is symbolic. The anointing, strategy and blessing of God is found in the cluster—the joining together of His people.

## The Housing Bubble Will Burst Again

We will also see the housing market at one of the best highs that has been seen in a generation, and then there will be a sudden drop. At that time people will ask, "Has the housing bubble burst again?"

Yes, and this housing bubble crisis will be different from the one we experienced in 2008. In many ways, this one will be worse. Some homeowners will be displaced, while others will experience plummeting home values. It will be a time to remember that our trust is not in possessions or wealth. Our trust is in the Lord our God.

This crisis will be detrimental and will have lasting effects. Out of the crisis, however, innovation in the housing market will be birthed. A new wave of developers and low-cost homes will emerge. The standard of housing will change, although the sizes of some homes will be greatly reduced. These new homes will be more energy efficient.

At this time, there will be a great redistribution of land, which will switch hands. This will mark a period of transition and transfer in the market.

## A Spiritual Famine in the Land

In this new era of time, not only will we see natural disasters and famine, but the world will also experience a spiritual famine. Many churches that have strayed away from Christ-centered ministry and have failed to maintain a hunger and passion for God and pursuing His heart will see a decline.

Although there will be conferences, special events, concerts and revival meetings galore, many of these gatherings will be absent of the presence of God. In the midst of the LED walls covered in eye-catching graphics, and the virtual backgrounds that exude professionalism and excellence, something will be missing. In the midst of the talented singers with the right harmonies and accompanying chords, with the perfect lyrics, melody and the most skillful worship bands, something will be missing.

For many years, we have ridden the waves of the anointings, mantles and words from a previous season, which were so powerful that without effort they could create a lasting impression for generations to come. Now, as the great revivals that we saw in the nineties have faded, and as the powerful reverberations of the prophetic services in the early 2000s are becoming a distant memory, there is a hollow sound in many churches. The moves of God of the past were birthed through intense prayer, fasting and passionate worship. Without those components, there can be no real move of God. Many have substituted a simple, quiet nod of meditation for fervent prayer. Just picking one thing to stop indulging in has been substituted for fasting and giving up food. And edgy performances and melodious tunes have been substituted for passionate, tearful, heartfelt worship. None of these things impress God. He simply wants a heart that is surrendered to Him.

In the days ahead, people will search for a revival and prophetic move of God in the trendy conferences and the latest fads that have been called revivals, but they will not find Him there. There was a time decades ago where you could find a church service on just about any corner. As long as the people there were naming the name of Christ and preaching the Word of God, you could experience an outpouring of

God's Spirit in your life. In America and among the nations, those experiences will be harder to come by for some. God is not always dwelling in what seems big. You may not always be able to find Him in the crowd, but you can always find Him in the cloud (see Exodus 13:21). Often, the new big will actually be small. There will be tangible moves of God in houses, hole-in-the-wall churches and unconventional gatherings. People may not find God in the usual places where they have been used to experiencing Him.

The spiritual famine that is already brewing now will show up even more in the coming days. It will not just be an absence of the glory of God in churches and so-called Spirit-filled meetings. It will be a famine for *hearing* the Word of God, a famine like that spoken of in Amos 8:11–12:

> "Behold, the days are coming," says the Lord GOD, "That I will send a famine on the land, not a famine of bread, nor a thirst for water, but of hearing the words of the LORD. They shall wander from sea to sea, and from north to east; they shall run to and fro, seeking the word of the LORD, but shall not find it."

In the time of Amos, it was a famine that the Lord Himself sent upon the people because of their disobedience. He stopped up their ears so that they could not hear, because at a time when they could hear, they would not listen. The coming spiritual famine will be a famine of hearing. Because the world has become so noisy with distractions everywhere, many people can no longer tune in to the voice of God. There are so many frequencies now that fight for our attention. Daily it is a battle between smartphones, iPads, TV shows, movies, social media and so much more. Everything is fighting to get your attention. Because of these distractions, many people's spiritual hearing will be stopped up. In addition, there is a generation of religious people who have become disobedient to the prodding of God's Spirit. They know the Word and can quote Scriptures, but they are fractured in the area of their love walk with the Lord. Because of their disobedience, they will not be able to hear God's words or His Word.

The Word of God is always accessible and in abundance, but can you hear it? The word *hearing* in Amos 8:11 is the Hebrew word *shama*. It means "to hear intelligently; to obey." We know that we are hearing God's Word when our actions line up with what we have heard. In the Hebrew language, hearing is not just being able to understand a phrase or sound audibly; hearing means obedience. The way we gauge our spiritual hearing is always through our level of obedience.

## Your Prophetic Goshen

Joseph carried the wisdom for Pharaoh, Egypt and Israel, and through his plan he even helped many of the surrounding nations. By God's wisdom, he knew exactly what to do. First was the matter of his family members who were still in Canaan and were suffering greatly from the famine. When his brothers in desperation journeyed to Egypt because of the famine, they found Joseph. He was now governing Egypt and overseeing the country's response to the food crisis.

Because of the process Joseph had gone through and the favor of God on his life, however, his brothers did not even recognize him. Genesis 42:8 says, "So Joseph recognized his brothers, but they did not recognize him." It is possible that God can do such a transformational work in your life that people from your old season don't recognize you in your new season. The favor of God is transformational.

Ultimately, after a series of tests Joseph revealed himself to his family and reunited with them. He was not angry with his brothers for what they had done to him. He realized it was the plan of God to preserve them. Look at his wise insight in Genesis 45:4–7:

> And Joseph said to his brothers, "Please come near to me." So they came near. Then he said: "I am Joseph your brother, whom you sold into Egypt. But now, do not therefore be grieved or angry with yourselves because you sold me here; for God sent me before you to preserve life. For these two years the famine has been in the land, and there are still five years in which there will be neither plowing nor harvesting. And God sent me before you to preserve a posterity for you in the earth, and to save your lives by a great deliverance."

After this powerful restoration between them, Joseph had the authority to gather his family from Canaan, bring them to Egypt and provide a place for them. He placed them in the land of Goshen. The exact location of Goshen is disputed. It was most likely a region along the Nile River that was conducive to farmers and herdsman. Goshen was a hidden gem and was described as the best land in Egypt. It was the most suitable for livestock and crops. Joseph placed them in this land in part because shepherds or farmers were looked down on in Egyptian culture. By placing them in the land of Goshen, he was able to keep them separate from that foreign culture—protecting them and keeping them close to him.

In the midst of the famine, Israel's children had all that they needed. Likewise, in the midst of famine, shortages, droughts and even economic collapse, you will dwell in your prophetic land of Goshen. If you can believe the words of the Lord, you will prosper in the midst of famine. The Spirit of God showed me an impactful vision of the coming famine in the world, but also that there would be safe haven places that would have resources in excess throughout the nations. Some Christians will be raised up to manage their own farms, producing their own food. Some will have stores and storehouses. Many believers will have successful businesses that will fund the Kingdom of God. Some will be in the financial sector, while others will be in the tech industries. I saw prophetic believers at the helm of some of the greatest innovations the world has ever seen.

Your prophetic Goshen is a place where you will labor with ease and without travail. It is a spiritual place of protection, provision and productivity. The exact meaning of the name *Goshen* is uncertain. Possibly, it is based on an Arabic root that means "cultivated" or "to labor." Some sources translate it as "drawing near."[2] Many people will be baffled at how, in the middle of the worst famine season, God's remnant will survive. God is not just going to cause you to survive; it will be your time to thrive.

Although I have released the prophecy of a coming severe famine, an agriculture crisis and food shortages like we have never seen, it is not meant to panic you. It is meant to prepare you. The prophetic word over your life is that no matter how bad those situations become, you will prosper in them. God always finds a way to provide for those whom He has chosen. Expect provision, financial release and resources to come into your hands from some of the most unexpected sources.

Just as God used Joseph to place his family in the best land in Egypt, so shall you dwell in the best land. You will see supernatural increase in the days, months and years to come.

## YOUR PROPHETIC FORECAST

Joseph had a prophetic plan for the famine that was coming in his time, and you need one, too! Joseph sought the Lord for His wisdom, and wisdom was given to him. God informed Joseph through Pharaoh's dream that the famine would be so great that the years of plenty that came before it would be forgotten. Through a word of wisdom, Joseph gave prophetic instructions to Pharaoh. Here are the six principles that we can derive from Joseph's plan in Genesis 41:33–36:

1. *Joseph interpreted Pharaoh's dream.*

   Interpreting Pharaoh's dream is symbolic of identifying a crisis that will arise in the future and charting out the path to navigate it. In your personal life, you will need to assess the condition of your own economy. The word *economy* comes from the Greek word *oikonomíā*, and it means "the state or condition of a house, or to manage a house."[3] How well you manage your house determines your personal economy, so you must determine what the state of your financial and spiritual well-being is. The Lord will always give you signs or prophetic pointers to show you when there is a disaster ahead. We just don't always catch those signs. Ask God for clarity, wisdom and acuity of vision to see the signs that point to what is ahead. God may show you in a dream or release a prophetic word through someone else that will help give you direction for your future.

2. *Joseph suggested selecting a discerning and wise man to place over the land of Egypt.*

   Through God's intelligence, Joseph instructed that a wise man be placed over Egypt to enforce and carry out the prophetic plan. This prophetically speaks of partnerships. Pharaoh could not save Egypt on his own. He needed someone who possessed a skill he did not. He rightfully chose Joseph for this huge task. The leader of Egypt needed someone who was a good financial steward, was trustworthy, walked in integrity and was aligned with God. Likewise, if you don't have the wisdom to manage what God has placed in your hands, you must pull on the skill sets of others. If you don't have the discipline to save and steward your finances, hire the services of people who do. It will be valuable for you in the days ahead.

Whom you partner with is paramount to your success. Sometimes God will use unlikely partnerships such as that between Pharaoh and Joseph. Pharaoh was not a believer in the God of Israel. He actually worshiped the sun god and possibly other false deities. In spite of this, Joseph's assignment was not to convert Pharaoh; his assignment was to preserve Israel through the resources of Egypt. There are many times throughout Scripture where the Lord used something unclean to provide wealth and resources for His people. Similarly, God may send people into your life who have the knowledge and skill that will help advance His agenda in your life, even if those people do not know the Lord. You must discern when your assignment is to minister to a person, and when it is to partner with him or her to transfer wealth to the Body of Christ (or even when it is to do both).

3. *Joseph advised appointing officers over the land.*

Joseph gave instructions to assign officers over the land to carry out the countrywide savings plan that had been set forth. We can learn from this example of stewardship and management. No plan that you implement can work unless you build a system or a strategy around it. Delegating assignments and appointing people and resources are important to the success of any budget, goal or endeavor. Psalm 90:12 says, "Teach us to number our days, that we may gain a heart of wisdom." The word *number* here means in Hebrew "to appoint or assign." Wisdom comes in organization. The glory of God is revealed through proper order. Creating systems is biblical and wise to do.

4. *Joseph urged that Pharaoh collect one fifth of the produce of the land.*

The most crucial part of Joseph's prophetic foreknowledge from God was to create a strategic savings plan. The prophet told Pharaoh to collect the fifth part of the produce from the land. In modern times, you can use this same God-given strategy to prosper in your life. A fifth part is 20 percent of your earnings or increase. The key is to initiate this savings plan when there is increase and things are going well. God's prophetic word allows us to be proactive and prepare ahead of time. What a brilliant plan from Joseph, to collect 20 percent during the prosperous times. This is the Joseph model.

5. *Joseph advised that Pharaoh gather the grain and store it up.*

After collecting a fifth part of the produce and grain of the land, there had to be a plan for storing it. It makes no sense to save if you are going to keep spending or using what you have saved. You must store up what is necessary. You are coming into a gathering season. You are entering a period of harvest. The word *harvest* means "to gather or store up."[4] Whenever the Lord places you in a harvest time, it is a prophetic signal to store up.

6. *Joseph directed that the reserve was to be distributed during the famine.*

This is the instruction of God. You must rightfully appropriate what you have saved. In days of spiritual or natural famine, distribute your reserve wisely. Allocating resources properly is not to be taken lightly. The biblical principle of stewardship deals with managing, growing and allocating money or resources well. It is important to pray for the skill, gift and discipline of managing and distributing resources wisely.

 **PROPHETIC HOPE**

In Genesis 26:12, Isaac sowed in the midst of a severe famine, and the Lord blessed him and prospered him. God's people have been ordained to prosper and thrive in adversarial environments. You will prosper and thrive in the midst of shortages in the world. The angels of the Lord are assigned to bring you into wealthy places. Not only will you see the Lord moving in the natural; you will also experience a prosperity of peace in your soul. When difficult times arise, you will rest in God.

# 8

# Technology Resurgence

But as for you, Daniel, conceal these words and seal up the book until the end of time; many will go back and forth, and knowledge will increase.

Daniel 12:4 NASB

At the end of 2019, I stood in a service in the church I pastor and shared the words of the Lord, who said to me, *The next decade will usher in a technology resurgence. There will be another tech boom in the world, and you must embrace the changes that are coming. They are going to change the way you do life from this point on.*

The Holy Spirit allowed me to know that we are on the verge of another breakout in technology, and it is going to create new methods, vehicles and platforms to get the message of the Gospel out to a new generation of people who do not know Him. These are the changes the Holy Spirit was referring to that we are to embrace.

We have seen how the pandemic that started in 2020 brought everything to a virtual platform, and the world connected in a way that we had not seen before. This, however, is nothing in comparison to what we are about to see in the coming years. This is the beginning of a new wave of technology. To some people it is both exciting and scary at the same time. What does another tech boom look like? What does a technology resurgence mean? Let's explore this.

## Artificial Intelligence

I know you have seen artificial intelligence, or AI, in futuristic movies, or have watched it in your favorite TV shows, or have read about it in books. But it will become a reality in the days ahead. Artificial intelligence is rapidly on the rise, and we will see it integrated into the world systems. In my times of prayer, the Lord has shown me glimpses of this kind of future—this new era and new order in the world. Prophetically speaking, we are about to see a new frontier of technology.

Some people would ask me, "Why would God speak to you concerning technology and artificial intelligence? Isn't prophecy just for edification, comfort and exhortation?" My answer is yes, those are the functions of prophecy, according to 1 Corinthians 14:3 (which we will come back to in a moment). But I would also answer that God would do or allow nothing in the earth without first revealing it to His servants the prophets, according to Amos 3:7. God shares these types of things with us because we are His chosen people, and He has given us the advantage. Literally, we carry the future within our spirits, and God will not allow us to be caught off guard concerning the major changes in the world, if we avail ourselves to Him.

To prepare the Church for a new world and new era that is now upon us, God spoke to me concerning the next technological boom and the rise of artificial intelligence. Again, God wants us as believers to be ahead of what is happening so that we are not caught off guard, and technology is an important area in which we are going to see massive change. So what is artificial intelligence? AI is the ability of computers, or of machines or robots controlled by computers, to perform the tasks that an intelligent being performs. These complex AI systems have human characteristics and will soon be a major presence at the forefront of manufacturing and in many of the occupations that people currently fill.

I also saw by the Spirit of God that the military will begin to use artificial intelligence as a key part of its programs. The next major war will even be fought with AI, in addition to soldiers with boots on the ground. Many of these advanced AI creations already exist but are hidden from the public eye.

You and I will see the revealing of a new wave of artificial intelligence in the coming years. These machines will be programmed to learn, problem solve and use intelligent reasoning. In the future, they will even be programmed to feel. Yes, I do believe that some of the new AI creations will even be sentient beings.

### Secure in God's Future Map

Paul told us in 1 Corinthians 14:3 that "he who prophesies speaks edification and exhortation and comfort to men." In this context, he was addressing personal prophecy, but this applies beyond that as well, to other forms of prophecy. There are several forms of prophecy: personal prophecy, corporate prophecy (to a congregation or group), governmental prophecy (to or concerning a government), national prophecy (concerning a country) and even global prophecy concerning the world.

What we see evident in the Bible is that within these forms or categories I just listed are also differing types of prophecy. These different types include prophetic instruction, warning prophecies, prophecies that reveal a person's calling, prophecies of correction, prophecies that reveal world events, and so much more. There is a clear difference between a prophetic word and just an encouraging word. The key difference is that prophecy reveals the future. The word *prophecy* means to foretell—to tell of a thing before it occurs.

The foundation of true prophecy is the Lord Jesus Christ. As Revelation 19:10 says, "The testimony of Jesus is the spirit of prophecy." Prophecy should ultimately point us back to Him. Let's take a moment to dissect Paul's statement that we just read in 1 Corinthians 14:3: "He who prophesies speaks edification and exhortation and comfort to men."

1. *Edification* in this verse is the Greek word *oikodome* and means "the act of building up." That is, to build someone up by the word of prophecy. Further, it comes from a compound Greek word meaning "architecture—to structure or build upon something." Prophecy is not just given to build you up; it is given for you to build with and upon. As we receive God's words concerning the future, they are given to us so that we have the advantage of building and planning around them.

   In 2 Peter 1:19 (KJV) we are told, "We have also a more sure word of prophecy; whereunto ye do well that ye take heed, as unto a light that shineth in a dark place, until the day dawn, and the day star arise in your hearts." The word *sure* in the text is the Greek word *bebaios*. It means "stable, trusty and firm." It comes from a root word meaning "that which is secure enough to walk on or step on." It is the idea that true prophecy is so sure that one can build on it. God reveals the future to us, His Ekklesia (those who believe in the Lord Jesus Christ), so that we can plan, prosper, strategize and build in order to advance His Kingdom.

2. *Exhortation* is a powerful part of prophecy. Because the Greek language is more three-dimensional than the English language, the original biblical text of 1 Corinthians 14:3 was a challenge to translate into our language. The biblical word *exhort* here has more of a layered meaning than our simple English word *exhort*. It is the Greek word *paraklesis*, and it means "a calling near, to summon." It also means "importation, as in bringing goods, services or re-sources from one place to another," and it means "persuasive discourse that is instructive, admonitory and encouraging." The religious Church has over-simplified this word to mean only encouragement, but as you see, there is so much more to it. Through the meaning of this word, we understand that Paul is telling the Church that prophecy summons us as believers into the mind and will of God. It is instruc-tive, providing direction and detail for the future. Ad-ditionally, when you receive prophecy, it is transfer-ring or importing spiritual resources into your life to prosper you.

3. *Comfort* is the Greek word *paramuthia*. It means "any address, whether made for the purpose of persuading, or of arousing and stimulating, or of

calming and consoling."[1] Through prophetic utterance, the peace of God comforts you. True prophecy gives you the ability to rest assured in knowing that God already has the future mapped out. He is ordering your steps, and your future is secure.

## Vision of Wearable Technology

God showed Daniel the prophet so far into the future that he saw things that were "unlawful" even to speak of in the age in which he lived. In other words, the things he saw were so contrary to the culture of his time, the way of life, the governmental structures and world affairs that God would not even allow him to reveal them. Daniel was able to see thousands of years into a world that he would never experience. In fact, he saw into the world that we currently live in. God revealed to him that as the time draws near to the culmination of all things, knowledge will increase. God carried Daniel so far into the future that He made him close the book and conceal it: "But as for you, Daniel, keep these words secret and seal up the book until the end of time; many will roam about, and knowledge will increase" (Daniel 12:4 NASB). Daniel was seeing into a heavenly scroll of prophecy and revelation that was incomprehensible to the human mind and that was not ready to be revealed for ages yet to come.

God was speaking to Daniel of the information age that we have been living in. There has been such a boom of information, media and social content. Information is now the most valuable commodity in the world. It is literally worth more than the price of gold, silver and other precious metals.

The tech and information age has made information so readily accessible. We are now in an age where the masses demand knowledge at their fingertips. Out of this will emerge a boom of wearable technology and eventually technology that is integrated with the human body. This will become a multibillion-dollar industry. I even saw in a vision where tech was integrated into different parts of the human body. Using this kind of tech, doctors will have the ability to monitor a person's vitals and condition from within. Individuals will be able to track their own levels, too. Bulky smartphones will be a thing of the past, as wearable and integrated smartphones will not just be at a person's fingertips but will literally be in them.

In the tech vision from God, I could also see the letter *E* and a logo, but I could not make out the full name of a new tech company that will pioneer and be groundbreaking in this integrated technology. At the time that these things accelerate, many believers will say that these technological advances are the mark of the beast, but they are not. Yet they are part of a beast-type system being constructed in the earth.

## The Spirit of the Age

As the world changes and technology increases, so will the persecution of the Church. Technology itself is neither bad nor good. It takes on the heart of the person who wields it. While many of the coming advances will be used for good, some will become the epicenter for diabolical agendas and antichrist systems. The spirit of antichrist is already here and is prevalent on the earth. Antichrist is anything opposed to or other than Christ. That is the spirit of the age. The current culture's absence of morals, its polluted politics on the left and the right, and its secular humanistic ideals have invaded and, in many ways, now dominate society.

115

The dismantling of many Christian beliefs in developed countries has not been done just by wicked leaders in high governmental places. It has also been done at the hands of religious leaders who have been polluted with politics and have been given over to their own self-seeking agendas. Nevertheless, as people's dependence on technology and convenience grows, we will see many more who will lose their need for God and His principles. This is dangerous!

In the near future, some of the new technologies will be used for stricter controls and even more censoring like nothing we have seen. Because of the monitoring capabilities on social media and other platforms, many Christians will not be allowed to share their beliefs and values. Portions of Scripture will be banned from being preached and released through these modes. Yet the Church will combat and overthrow the spirit of the age by infiltrating every area of society, every industry and every system. Our mission is to be the light of God in a dark place. It will not be through our sharp rhetoric or angry responses to persecution that we will have victory. We have already been given victory, and the end of the story has already been written. Rather, it will be through our stance for righteousness—living out the Word and loving everyone in spite of the persecution and demonic use of technology—that we will win.

### Business in the Tech Resurgence

The tech boom that we will see is going to stimulate the economies of key nations. New millionaires will emerge because of their investments in the companies producing new tech products while they are in their infancy. God said to me that we will see emerging markets begin to rise and take center stage in the world of business. I saw the countries of Russia, Taiwan, India and South Africa, and saw where new industrial initiatives will be undertaken in these regions. India and Africa will become distribution hubs.

For the past several decades, China has served as a distribution hub for the world. Chinese businesses have created and exported food items, pharmaceuticals and even gadgets and smart devices. In the near future, I saw the distribution hub shift from China and go to some of the developing countries that I mentioned. Currently these countries' markets may be volatile, but the day is coming when they will rise. Although China is poised to lead among the nations, it will no longer function or export in the same way that it has in the past.

As these shifts occur, get ready to see major changes in the business world among the nations. People will migrate to the new areas as new tech and business hubs are established in different cities. Many people will leave the areas that they live in and completely uproot to follow the money trails created by this resurgence.

 **YOUR PROPHETIC FORECAST**

The world of technology is already quite vast. But the words God has given me regarding a technology resurgence paint a picture of our being pushed ahead by leaps and bounds. Life as we know it will change, along with everything around us. Where does this leave you in the middle of these unstoppable changes? Many people are afraid of these changes because they fear adapting or fear getting lost in the shuffle. But you are not going to get lost in changing times. You have the advantage because you are receiving the words of the Lord ahead of time, to prepare you. You will navigate what is

ahead with grace and ease. Here are some takeaways to help
you navigate the coming tech boom:

- The technology resurgence will revitalize the economies of key nations and create new opportunities for
  employment.
- You will have the opportunity to be part of this resurgence. For that reason, you may want to learn new
  skill sets in the field of technology. Don't be afraid to
  explore something that you have never done before.
- In the new era, some degree fields will almost become
  obsolete. Post-graduate classes, training and studies
  in key areas will be beneficial for the way that the
  world is moving.
- Keep your eyes on these jobs because they will be
  the future: data science and analysis, programming,
  cybersecurity, robotics engineering, biotechnology,
  autonomous vehicles and devices, and so much more.

## PROPHETIC HOPE

Heaven is releasing Kingdom technology into your hands in
the form of spiritual gifts and expressions from God. Heavenly technology is being downloaded into your spirit to empower you to accomplish all that God has given you to do.
While the world is advancing in natural, human knowledge,
you will advance in the ways of the Holy Spirit. The Holy
Spirit will empower you through Jesus Christ to do what you
could not do in your own human ability. You will experience
supernatural and prophetic intelligence from heaven to align
with God's agenda in the earth.

9

# Unusual Weather Patterns

Fire and hail, snow and clouds; stormy wind, fulfilling His word . . .

Psalm 148:8 NASB

Because of the prophetic times that we live in, we will see what we have never seen before. Due to the earth's volatility, the weather on the horizon will break records, make history and set new benchmarks. Romans 8:22 reveals that the earth and the whole of creation is groaning in labor pains. The earth is constantly going through major shifts. For this reason, we will see some of the most unusual weather patterns in the days ahead.

There has always been a unique relationship between God's prophets and the weather and its elements. Instances of this are sprinkled throughout the Bible. For instance, God used Elijah to shut up the heavens so that there would be no rain for a few years: "And Elijah the Tishbite, of the inhabitants of Gilead, said to Ahab, 'As the Lord God of Israel lives, before whom I stand, there shall not be dew nor rain these years, except at my word'" (1 Kings 17:1). In this passage, God used drought and the lack of rain pronounced by Elijah as an omen to Baal worshipers. This was a supernatural weather disruption.

In Baal worship, the archenemy of their god Baal was Mot. This archenemy was known as the god of death, infertility and drought, whereas Baal was known as the rain god that brought fertility to the land.[1] According to myth, an epic battle took place between these two gods. When Elijah closed the heavens and stopped the rain, the Baal worshipers were distraught because to them it meant that their god had been vanquished by Mot. The Lord used their weather crisis to prophesy the end of an era of Baal rulership. Elijah taunted them concerning their false god Baal. No matter how hard they prayed to him and performed their rituals, he would not answer. Elijah made it clear that it was not the false gods Baal or Mot that controlled the rain and drought—it is the God of Israel who controls the weather.

In Scripture, various weather phenomena were a common occurrence. We see many examples of this from Old Testament to New Testament. In Acts 27, the apostle Paul was a prisoner being taken to Rome. He had been placed in prison for preaching the Gospel. A centurion took Paul and other prisoners aboard a ship. Paul perceived prophetically that the trip would end in disaster. He warned his fellow travelers about it, but the centurion in charge of the prisoners decided to continue with the journey, so they set sail. Verses 13–16 tell us,

> When the south wind blew softly, supposing that they had obtained their desire, putting out to sea, they sailed close by

Crete. But not long after, a tempestuous head wind arose, called Euroclydon. So when the ship was caught, and could not head into the wind, we let her drive. And running under the shelter of an island called Clauda, we secured the skiff with difficulty.

A Euroclydon is comparable to a cyclone with hurricane-force winds. It is a tempestuous northeast wind that blows in the Mediterranean. It can also be compared to a typhoon.[2] In other words, this was a massive storm that devoured the ship Paul was on. He announced to the guards and other prisoners that their lives would not be lost, but that the ship would be. After fourteen nights of battling the insane winds and waves of the Euroclydon, they finally saw land. When they were shipwrecked near Malta, the centurion had the prisoners jump overboard. They used boards and other pieces of the ship to float to land.

### The Earth Is in Travail

God used this unusual weather and crazy storm to bring Paul to the island of Malta, where he healed a man of dysentery and healed many others who were diseased. We see through this that often, nature's disruption is God's intervention. Ultimately, it is God who governs the weather and all things in the earth. Nature, however, can be volatile. This is exacerbated even more in our time due to the birth pangs the earth is now experiencing. The closer the earth moves to its own redemption, the more volatile things will become. Now more than ever, we will see this volatility manifested in the seasons. Dramatic changes will occur that cause the seasons and their rotations to collide. More and more, one season will carry the traits of another—unusual warm weather in winter and unprecedented cool periods in summer.

When you see these things, understand that it is the earth in great travail. Yes, the earth is signaling the emergence of God's sons and daughters. The word *travail* means painful or laborious work or effort.[3] The clearest picture of travail is a woman giving birth to a child. Before she can experience the joy of her beautiful baby, she must go through a period of great pain and agony. That period is travail or labor. But the good thing is, after the labor comes the birth. In many ways, the earth is going through agony and pain due to the corruption on it. Corruption, wickedness and iniquity affect the earth's balance. In this new era, as we see many unusual weather-related records being set, some of this weather will be disastrous because of the great travail and imbalance in the earth.

I saw a vison of a massive tsunami hitting the Asia Pacific region again. This will be even more devastating than what took place in 2004 with the Indian Ocean tsunami. But the Lord said to me that at that time, we will see the message of the Gospel accelerate in the Asian nations even more. Although God is not the cause of these devastating acts, He never allows devastation without allowing something beautiful to emerge.

Massive, super hurricanes will continue to develop and affect the United States and other countries. America will enter a period of great shakings. It will be nothing like we have ever seen so far in our modern times. In the Spirit, I saw the fault lines throughout the earth on what appeared to be a world map. There was much shifting and activity. The tectonic plates will begin to shift, and we will see more significant earthquakes throughout the earth. Specifically, the Americas will be shaken by these high-magnitude earthquakes.

In addition, I saw great winds blowing with unprecedented velocity and speed. Over the coming months and years, many people will note how out of the ordinary the weather is. It will be a sign to the Church that the time is drawing closer for a great reveal of God's glory.

## The Biblical Meaning of Weather

The Bible contains much prophetic symbolism. God speaks through everything. In 1 Corinthians 2:15 (AMP) we read, "But the spiritual man [the spiritually mature Christian] judges all things [questions, examines and applies what the Holy Spirit reveals], yet is himself judged by no one [the unbeliever cannot judge and understand the believer's spiritual nature]." Those who are spiritually mature and in tune with the Holy Spirit have an understanding of how the spiritual world affects the natural.

Verse 14 of 1 Corinthians 2 says, "But the natural man does not receive the things of the Spirit of God, for they are foolishness to him; nor can he know them, because they are spiritually discerned." Some things can only be discerned by the Spirit. They make no natural sense to others. To the spiritual, all things are spiritual. The pure in heart can detect God through and in anything. In Scripture, God speaks through weather-related occurrences. Here are the prophetic meanings of various elements of the weather:

### *The Hail*

Hail is referenced several times throughout the Bible. In Exodus 9:18 the Lord warns Pharaoh through Moses, "Behold, tomorrow about this time I will cause very heavy hail to rain down, such as has not been in Egypt since its founding until now." At times in biblical history, hail is sign of God's judgment on the affairs of humanity. This does not mean that every time it hails there is judgment. Symbolically, however, hail represents God's judgment and correction, balancing the scales. When we see hail, it is a reminder that God is governing the cosmos. It is He who corrects wrongs and sets the earth in order.

Revelation 16:21 says, "And great hail from heaven fell upon men, each hailstone about the weight of a talent. Men blasphemed God because of the plague of the hail, since that plague was exceedingly great." These are the words of John when he was on the Isle of Patmos. He saw many visions of the future and what was to come. Specifically in this passage, he saw hail of massive size falling on people. According to Scripture, the hail is an accompaniment of one of the plagues that will be released upon the earth in the last days.

### The Rain

In the Old Testament, rain was attributed to the blessing of God. Deuteronomy 28:12 says, "The LORD will open to you His good treasure, the heavens, to give the rain to your land in its season, and to bless all the work of your hand. You shall lend to many nations, but you shall not borrow." Because the ancient world was run by a system of agriculture, rain was necessary to live. Cities and civilizations were only as strong as their military defense and the crops that they produced. Without rain, there would be no cultivating of crops. This meant there would be no food. The abundance of rain or an unfortunate drought often determined the rise and fall of ancient cities.

Deuteronomy 11:17 shows that when God's people were in rebellion, He would withhold rain from them to correct the error of their ways: "Lest the LORD's anger be aroused against you, and He shut up the heavens so that there be no rain, and the land yield no produce, and you perish quickly from the good land which the LORD is giving you." If His people were obedient, they would eat the good of the land. If they were disobedient, then their crops would fail due to lack of rain.

The same blessing of rain appears in the New Testament. Hebrews 6:7 states, "For the earth which drinks in the rain that often comes upon it, and bears herbs useful for those by whom it is cultivated, receives blessing from God." God blesses the earth with rain. Prophetically, rain is symbolic of the blessing of God on His people. In addition, rain represents the refreshing of God. It depicts being filled and overflowing with abundance. When the heavens produce rain, it means that they are open. An open heaven is a sign of the release of God's answers, blessings and treasures upon His people.

### The Snow

Psalm 147:16 says, "He gives snow like wool; He scatters the frost like ashes." Snow is mentioned 23 times in Scripture. Many of the verses use the phrase *white as snow*. Psalm 51:7 speaks of God's cleansing even beyond the whiteness of snow: "Purge me with hyssop, and I shall be clean; wash me, and I shall be whiter than snow." It is clear by the Word of God that snow is symbolic of purity.

Naturally, when it snows, the snow clears the air of impurities and harmful substances that could be in the atmosphere. As it is in the natural, so it is in the Spirit. I have seen God blanket regions that He is bringing purity to with abnormal snow. Sometimes He is cleansing wickedness and corruption out of governments, and other times He is calming unrest in the people. Some cities and states have patterns that show that when the summer comes, crime increases, but when the winter comes with its snow, the people are relegated to their houses and crime decreases.

Further, it is the blood of Jesus that washes us whiter than snow. We are cleansed by His blood. We are renewed by His purifying blood. The clearest picture the Bible gives of this cleansing is snow. When we see snow, it is a reminder of God's righteousness and how He desires to purify the nations.

### Lightning and Thunder

Lightning starts as static electricity. It is electrical discharge that occurs within the clouds, and it is caused by imbalances between the atmosphere and the ground. Lightning shows up as a quick flash of light. It is extremely hot and heats the air around it to a degree five times hotter than the surface of the sun. When this happens, it causes the surrounding air to expand rather rapidly and vibrate, producing the crashing sound of thunder that we hear shortly after a lightning strike.[4]

During the time when Moses was leading the millions of Israelites, God came down to speak with him and the people, giving them the Ten Commandments. This was such a scary experience for the people that in Exodus 20:18–21 they begged Moses to have God speak only to him instead, and then he could relate God's message to them afterward:

> Now all the people witnessed the thunderings, the lightning flashes, the sound of the trumpet, and the mountain smoking; and when the people saw it, they trembled and stood afar off. Then they said to Moses, "You speak with us, and we will hear; but let not God speak with us, lest we die."
>
> And Moses said to the people, "Do not fear; for God has come to test you, and that His fear may be before you, so that

you may not sin." So the people stood afar off, but Moses drew near the thick darkness where God was.

The lightning and thunder showed up in the cloud of glory that surrounded God and Moses. Thunder and lightning can be a sign of the awe-inspiring, great and terrible glory of God. When the people saw the thunder and lightning and God speaking out of the midst of the dark, thick cloud, they were terribly afraid.

Further, Luke 10:18–19 reveals Jesus describing for His disciples Satan's great fall: "I saw Satan fall like lightning from heaven. Behold, I give you the authority to trample on serpents and scorpions, and over all the power of the enemy, and nothing shall by any means hurt you." Here, lightning represents that judgment of God against His enemy. It also shows the symbolic transfer of the authority Jesus gives to the disciples to dominate over Satan and his cohorts.

### Solar Storms and Signs in the Sky

As unusual as this may sound, God said to me that over this decade we are in, we will see space weather and solar storms increase and show up more in the news. As these occurrences increase, they will affect the systems and grids of the earth. Furthermore, there will be strange and uncommon occurrences in the sky above that many experts will not be able to explain. These unexplainable signs will point to the prophetic time we are living in that is unfolding right before our eyes. Luke 21:25 explains this: "And there will be signs in the sun, in the moon, and in the stars; and on the earth distress of nations, with perplexity, the sea and the waves roaring." These signs will increase more and more in the coming months and years. You will know that God is speaking, and yes, even prophesying through the heavens.

##  YOUR PROPHETIC FORECAST

As I mentioned earlier, the earth is groaning, according to Romans 8:22. This travail is really contractions responding to heaven's call. In the times ahead, you will continue to see new weather-related records set and broken. Climates, temperatures and atmospheric weather will be unusual and at times quite alarming. Because of occurrences from super storms to tsunamis to unexplainable atmospheric phenomena, many people will stand in amazement—and at times in terror—of what they see happening on the face of the earth. But you will know that it is simply the earth giving birth. It is the shedding of the old, preparing for the new. And most importantly, it is a call to the sons and daughters of God to get into our positions. We do this by repentance, by coming into agreement with God's plan for our lives, and by being fully at His service to demonstrate the Gospel message in our unstable world.

Some people will see these unusual weather patterns as judgments from God, but most of these occurrences will not be judgments. Every time you see or hear of an unusual occurrence related to the weather, it is a mile marker in the Spirit signaling you as a believer to realize the urgency of walking in the fullness of your purpose with the Lord.

##  PROPHETIC HOPE

In Genesis 1:14, God said, "Let there be lights in the expanse of the heavens to separate the day from the night. And let them be for signs and for seasons, and for days and years" (ESV). Seasons are signs and mile markers that show forth God's divine plan in the earth. The Bible speaks of spring, summer, fall and winter, but then it speaks of a fifth spiritual season called *due season* (for example, see Leviticus 26:4 and Galatians 6:9). While the earth is experiencing unusual and even disruptive seasons, you will enter into your due season. A due season is a divinely appointed time on God's calendar where His promises will be fully realized and manifested in your life. Your due season is your sign that you are under an open heaven. Your prayers are unhindered, and God is releasing down His blessings in your life.

10

# Rebirth of the Media Industry

And this gospel of the kingdom will be preached in all the world as a witness to all the nations, and then the end will come.

Matthew 24:14

In my lifetime, I have seen so many changes to the world of media and how it influences society. *Media* is a broad term for the vehicles of mass communication. It includes broadcasting, publishing and the internet. Social media has exploded in a way that we could never have envisioned. Anything you need, from news to the latest updates in current culture, is literally at your fingertips.

It was just a short time ago that the Lord spoke to me about using the available media as a platform for ministry. So in the past year, I started a podcast called *Global Prophetic Forecast* on the Charisma Podcast Network. It exploded to a quarter of a million downloads in a matter of months. By the leading of the Spirit, God directed me to go live on social media on Mondays at 12 noon CST to share pressing prophetic directives, updates, prayer points and encouraging words to ignite those who would hear. Previously, I had no intention of doing this, nor did I have any desire to. I had received many words from God that I was supposed to go ahead with it, but to be honest, I kept delaying it.

Then, in one of my times of prayer, I finally told the Lord that I would obey and do what He had asked. I had no idea of the impact that those unscripted and unplanned prophetic moments would have on tens of thousands of people. In a month, there were nearly 2 million total views from my combined social media videos. As I began to share the truth of God's Word, I quickly saw that people were hungry for the Word.

There is a hunger for God, now more than ever. People want the pure Word, without gimmicks, tricks and man's made-up doctrine. People just want Jesus for real. As I stepped out to obey God in embracing my media ministry, the prayer requests and testimonies came pouring in by the thousands. My admin team could not keep up with all of the calls and messages. We had to hire more staff to help meet the demand. We would read messages and pray for people for hours. It was through this experience that God shared with me that the world would see a rebirth of the media industry.

**Deceptive Media**

For far too long, the media has been used as a diabolical tool to infiltrate homes and pervert the truth. The things that are allowed on mainstream TV are appalling. Many of these things are tainting innocent minds and opening them up to demonic possession. Because TV and other forms of media are portals that open spiritual doors through vision or hearing, people can be opening themselves up to anything just by viewing a particular show or listening to a particular podcast. The enemy has had a direct line into millions of homes through the media.

Not only have we seen the media pervert the minds of many in the next generation; we have also seen it divide people when it comes to government and politics. The media has been a mouthpiece; it can either inflame or deescalate situations and public reactions to them.

In addition, many media outlets have been used as a means of distracting people from the truth. With the manipulation of these platforms, shadow hands have been able to stir up people's emotions, trigger their actions and sadly, control their minds. This is not the will of God for the media. This is a type of witchcraft that has brought about one of the greatest deceptions in our modern times.

## The Kingdom of the Air

The media in and of itself is not evil. It is greatly dependent on the heart of the person using it. Like money, the media in its different forms will simply amplify the heart of the person who is creating the content. Because of the age of technology we are in, most forms of media are transmitted electronically through the airwaves. While there is much spiritual traffic traversing the airwaves, this is also true naturally. There is much media activity going on, from signals, to frequencies, to channels.

Why are the airways so important? Because they are the realm of spiritual warfare in the earth. Ephesians 2:2 explains that Satan has occupied this domain, "in which you once walked according to the course of this world, according to the prince of the power of the air, the spirit who now works in the sons of disobedience." The devil is called *the prince of the power of the air*. To everything within the cosmos God has given a certain power or ability. The word *power* in this Scripture text is *force*. The airways carry a massive force, and Lucifer traverses that aerial domain.

In the New International Version translation of Ephesians 2:2, the writer calls Satan *the ruler of the kingdom of the air*. The air is not just wind; it is spirit. The air is not just around us and above our heads; it is a kingdom. All kingdoms have magistrates or governing structures with rank and order, subordinates and subjects. Unfortunately, Satan does his most damaging work in and through the airways. For individuals, his attacks come as whispers in their minds through the air. For mass infiltration, he uses people who are demonically influenced, whose voices are amplified through broadcasting, television, social media and all the other forms of the media.

Nevertheless, as Christians we are not powerless when it comes to the kingdom of the air. As the apostle Paul so eloquently stated in Galatians 5:25, "If we live in the Spirit, let us also walk in the Spirit." We are called to live in the Spirit and walk in the Spirit. At its base definition, the word *air* in the Greek language is spirit. To walk in the Spirit and be fully given over to the Spirit of God is akin to the Greek word *pneumatikos*. It is one who walks, lives and is animated by the Holy Spirit.

This means that as believers, we have dominion in the kingdom of the air. The Bible may call Satan the prince of the power of the air, but it also calls us kings and priests in Revelation 1:6. Through Christ Jesus we are kings and priests, meaning we outrank Satan and his demons. So as a

Christian, you have a right to occupy every domain of the media. You have a right to speak into the airwaves and release the words of the Lord. As you do that, the powers of darkness that have been oppressing people will bow down to the authority of Jesus Christ within you.

## Dawn of a New Media Era

The world as we know it is on the cusp of one of the greatest media expansions we have ever seen. We will see new forms and platforms of media emerge. These communication-driven entities will connect the world in a closer way. Some television conglomerates that have led the way in previous decades will diminish in rank, viewership and size. I even see prophetically that a major TV and media company will split. This divide of the company will cause it to lose momentum.

The landscape of the media world will evolve and change drastically in this new era. A new social media platform will emerge that will rise above Facebook, Twitter, Instagram and the popular platforms that we currently see. At the onset, this new platform will be very controversial. People will be concerned about its governance and regulations. Nonetheless, it will grow rapidly. Young people will mobilize around it. Its emphasis, however, will not be on following people, as much as it will be on gaining access to people's access information. Individual people will be able to sell and monetize their own data.

This new platform that I see prophetically will mark the dawn of a new period in social media. News headlines will come across that focus on how social media is changing, and truly it is. Knowledge and information will increase as the way we do life and interconnect with one another morphs.

## Resurgence of Christian TV and Media

The media world will go through another rebirth of sorts, and in this period we will witness a massive resurgence of Christian television and media streams. Although some prognosticators have said that Christian media is on the decline, I heard the Lord speak to me that *Christian television and media will surge in this new era.*

New Christian programming and presentations will come forth that will be ideas from God designed to reach a generation of those who are unchurched. Using the skillful creativity of multimedia graphics, cinematography and state-of-the-art production, movies and shows will be created that reach people right where they are with the message of the Gospel. Yes, we have seen Christian movies and shows for many decades, but God is speaking of a surge that goes far beyond the things that we have seen.

A level of innovation is coming from those who pioneer in Christian media and TV that will be unparallel to anything we have seen before. God is raising up prophetic media forerunners who will embark on a new journey and pave the way for a new age of Christian media. Through this resurgence, Christian TV will come back front and center stage in a similar way to the popularity it had in the seventies, eighties and nineties. But this time, it will be enhanced by new streaming platforms, new faces and new voices. Because there will be an increasing hunger for God and a desire to know what is going on in the world, the preaching of the Gospel will be sought after once again. This Christian media resurgence will work hand in hand with the harvest of souls that we will see come into the Body of Christ. Many souls will be saved through this rebirth of the media.

## YOUR PROPHETIC FORECAST

*Media* in and of itself is such a broad term. It encompasses so much, from television to Snapchat. As much as its different platforms have been used negatively in many ways, they have also been used positively to impact the lives of many. The media is one of the greatest platforms of our day that can be used for reaching the lost and spreading the message of Jesus Christ. This does not have to be done by posting or propagating Bible verses. Spreading the message of Christ can be done through how we live and what we demonstrate through the media.

I find that the Lord is calling many people to engage in media, whether social media or a more traditional format, in order to represent Christ. One of the questions that I get from people is "How do I know if I'm called to the media?" Here are some of the signs that you have been called to impact others through the media:

- You have the gift of gab! In other words, you like to talk. You may be laughing at this one, but the gift of gab is a sure sign that God has given you the passion to talk so that He can use your voice.
- People are just naturally drawn to you. This could be a sign that you are called to influence others positively through communication or the media.
- You have a heavy interest in a certain form of media, for instance Instagram, podcasts, TV or some other format.
- You have a passion to write. Prophetic scribes are being raised up in this hour to write the heart of God and transmit it for others to read. Writing articles, books and the like is also part of the print or online media.

136

These are just a few signs to give you a jump start. They may help you recognize that God may want to use you through media outlets to spread His Word. In the coming days, we will witness a rebirth of the media, and you get to be part of it.

## PROPHETIC HOPE

God is amplifying your voice, your reach and your influence! You are the word from God that people will see demonstrated before their eyes. According to 2 Corinthians 3:2–3, you are a living epistle not written by ink, but by the Spirit of God. This means that people will read your life and see Jesus in and through you. For this reason, you carry a media anointing. You don't have to write a book, have a podcast or be interviewed on a TV show. You are the book that people will read and be drawn to Christ through because of your walk with the Lord.

# 11

# Supernatural Harvest

The harvest is the end of the age, and the reapers are the angels.

Matthew 13:39

When the Holy Spirit first commissioned me to begin doing prophetic evangelism in 2001, I did not know what I was doing at all. My relationship with God had grown stronger, however, and I had such a passion for His presence and Word. I have still managed to keep growing in that hunger till this day. Having a spiritual hunger and being available are the keys to God using you as a conduit to spread His message and anointing through you.

At that time in my life, the Lord would randomly tell me to walk up to strangers and give them a word of prophecy. My church leadership and other credible people had already recognized me as a prophet, but I did not yet fully operate in this office. And I was most comfortable ministering in a church setting. Then God completely turned my world upside down by telling me to go up to strangers in my everyday life and give them a word from the Lord. I had no idea that God was training me for what I would be doing in the future.

The first time I walked up to a stranger and shared a prophecy that the Lord had given me for that person, I was physically shaking. *What if this person laughs in my face? What if what I say is wrong? What if this person does not receive the word?* All these thoughts were in my head, screaming at me, but I did it anyway. The first person I approached looked at me like a deer in the headlights, in bewilderment. With tears, however, that person received the word from God. I was shocked.

This kind of scenario happened every day for several weeks. Finally, the Holy Spirit sent me to speak to someone who clearly was not open to anything about the Bible or God. This person was living an alternative lifestyle, was always dressed in somewhat eccentric fashion, and did strange and unusual things with piercings and tattoos. I did not know the person well, although we had crossed paths from time to time and I had never detected any meanness coming across— although not much pleasantness radiated my way either. God gave me a detailed word of knowledge and prophecy for this individual alone, whom I saw in the Spirit had been abused by a relative when younger. The resulting trauma had sent the person down an unwholesome path.

The Lord told me to say to this individual, "You need to forgive your abuser. And you need to know that God will heal you and change your life." At the moment, when I delivered that word from God, the tough facial expression I had always seen before melted away. With tears welling up and spilling over, this person asked for permission to hug me, and got it. Then we prayed together.

I walked away from that experience not quite understanding what had happened. I said to myself, *God, but I didn't have this individual pray the sinner's prayer. I didn't lead this person to You.*

God replied, *You planted a seed, and I will send others to water it.*

It was a year later that I ran into the same person again—except not the same. The quirky clothing was gone, along with some of the other unusual features and accessories. In their place was a shoulder bag that had *Jesus Christ* written on it, with Scriptures all across it. A complete change of lifestyle and appearance had taken place—a total transformation into a new creation (see 2 Corinthians 5:17). God reminded me that some of us plant the seed, others water the seed, but it is God who gives the increase. He used this experience to show me that these are the types of people who are about to come into the Kingdom of God. They are simply waiting on someone who is willing to get uncomfortable and go after the harvest.

## Vision of the Coming Harvest

I find that God loves using ordinary people to accomplish extravagant tasks. When the assignment is bigger than you, that is how you know it is from God. Everything God will ever mandate us to do, He makes sure we cannot accomplish in our own strength. The key component is faith. Faith is not just some abstract concept. Faith is belief put into action!

Can you believe that God wants to use you to usher in the next great move of the Spirit? God is not interested in mindless drones who all function the same way. He created each of us with different personalities and different giftings and assignments because we each have a part to play. The Holy

Spirit is interested in partnership. He wants to partner with you to accomplish His will in the earth. Isn't that amazing?

The Lord took me up into a vision, and I saw this massive field. There were all kinds of people in the field, with every culture and race represented. The odd thing about this vision is that the people in it—there had to be hundreds of thousands of them—were all carrying some form of tool or working instrument. They were worshiping God, but they were positioned as if they were ready to work. The Holy Spirit told me that the next great influx of people coming into the Kingdom are coming ready to work. We will see God do an accelerated process in many of their lives; they will mature quickly in their character and giftings.

A massive influx of souls will be saved in this coming harvest. Some of these people will be your family members, friends, co-workers and people who live in your neighborhood. The unusual thing about this next great harvest is that many of them will not come to Christ in a church building. The altar that they will meet Jesus at will be right there on your job, or in the coffee shop, grocery store or school. This next move of God cannot be limited to the confines of the four walls of your church building. People need Jesus every day, not just on Sundays for an hour and a half. Opportunities for salvation are going to show up in the most uncommon and unusual places, but this is the beauty of the next wave. It will be seen in believers rising up to be the Church in every community, city and sector of the world.

### The Harvest at the End of the Age

In Matthew 13:3–9, Jesus gives us the now famous parable of the sower. He shares that there was a farmer who went out to sow. As he sowed, several things happened. Some seeds fell by the wayside, meaning the footpath or road, and the birds ate them. Some seeds fell on stony ground that did not have quality soil or much earth. Those seeds sprang up immediately but had no depth and quickly withered away. Other seeds fell among thorns, and those thorns choked the life out of them. Then there were the seeds that fell on good ground and yielded a harvest—some thirty, sixty and even a hundred times what had been planted.

The disciples inquired about the meaning of this parable. They were also perplexed about why Jesus always spoke to them in such parables. Jesus explained that the parable was about hearing the Word of the Kingdom (see Matthew 13:10–23). He also told them to be careful how they were hearing (see Mark 4:24). The enemy comes as a thief to try to steal the words of the Lord out of people's hearts (ears). Not only have many people in this world been blinded, but their hearing hearts have also been compromised as the enemy steals from them in broad daylight.

Jesus goes on in Matthew 13:24–30 to tell the parable of the wheat and the tares, and then to explain it. He gives the example of the Kingdom of heaven being like a man who sowed good seeds in his field. During the night, the enemy came in and sowed tares. The wheat and the tares then had to grow up together, and at the time of harvest they could be separated. Jesus further explained this parable by saying,

He who sows the good seed is the Son of Man. The field is the world, the good seeds are the sons of the kingdom, but the tares are the sons of the wicked one. The enemy who sowed them is the devil, the harvest is the end of the age, and the reapers are the angels. Therefore as the tares are gathered and burned in the fire, so it will be at the end of this age.

Matthew 13:37–40

The more traditional translations say that the harvest is "at the end of the world." The word *world* there is the Greek word *ion*, meaning "an age." Some experts believe that *ion* or *age* means "a period of a thousand years." Every time we come to the end of an age, there is a new mega harvest. We have yet to see the full harvest of this current millennium. We have seen glimpses of it, but in the coming years we will see one of the greatest harvests ever to be recorded in Christian history.

**The Angels Are the Reapers**

According to Matthew 13:39, the angels are the reapers. God is sending angelic assistance to help bring in the harvest. Reaping angels are being sent on assignment to help us gather it in. It is through the angel armies of heaven that we will see an increase of the supernatural. Many people will be unaware that massive angels will be standing among us. The Bible calls them ministering spirits because they are sent to serve our Kingdom assignments in the earth.

In this coming harvest season, we must learn how to utilize and employ our angels to work on assignment with us. Sometimes they are sent to strengthen us for the work of ministry. Other times, they are coming for the words that we decree. There are specific angels who come because of and for what we have prayed. They gather our words and bring them up before the Father. Then they come bearing the answers to our prayers. In Daniel 10:12, an angel says to Daniel, "Do not fear, Daniel, for from the first day that you set your heart to understand, and to humble yourself before your God, your words were heard; and I have come because of your words." Angels are drawn to our words. So are demon spirits when we speak opposite of the Word of God.

One of the most powerful tools for unlocking the next harvest is prophecy. When you speak the Word of God, you are planting the heavens; you are establishing God's will in the earth. To plant the heavens means that you bring heaven's agenda and plans into this world by speaking forth what God has said (see Isaiah 51:16).

Psalm 103:20 sheds light on the ministry of angels surrounding the spoken Word of God: "Bless the LORD, you His angels, who excel in strength, who do His word, heeding the voice of His word." In this new era, we will see the angels of the Lord excelling in strength because of the increase of the Spirit of prophecy in the earth. This is why true prophetic utterance is so vital to the Church. Prophecy brings the Church strength. The word *excel* in this verse is the Hebrew word *gibbowr*. It literally means "powerful or warrior." In this context, it means "to become strong." As you speak the words of the Lord, the angels who are on assignment to you become stronger. They are warring in the heavenlies against demonic forces, and they harken to God's words.

## Prophetic Evangelism

Earlier, I mentioned the beginning of my journey years ago in passionate evangelism. What I learned in those days is just how much God wants to reveal His heart to people. God loves everyone so much, no matter their religion, background, culture or belief. Of course, many people are deceived because the god of this world has blinded their eyes. But the true and living God wants all people to come to Him.

As I began to move more heavily in winning souls, years ago the Lord gave me an idea to go to the mall in my city and take teams with me to minister. Because the mall was private, I warned those whom I was training of the risks that were involved. "The worst thing that could happen is that you could be arrested," I informed them. "But don't worry. I'll bail you out—or you might have to bail me out," I stated laughingly.

The people in this group were so passionate about God, but most of them were afraid of this level of evangelism. Most were terrified of being rejected. The Lord took me to a solution for this in His Word—a Scripture that I had read, quoted and rehearsed hundreds, if not thousands, of times. This time, the Holy Spirit said, *Look deeper*. The Scripture was Proverbs 11:30, "The fruit of the righteous is a tree of life, and he who wins souls is wise." The Spirit told me, *Focus on the word "win" in the text.*

I began studying this verse more deeply. Here, *win* is the Hebrew word *laqach*. Two main definitions stood out to me: "to accept and to receive." The original text, therefore, says that he who receives or accepts souls is wise. This was an epiphany to me. God did not want us to criticize these souls, analyze them or even in this case judge them. He was just asking us to *receive* them.

You see, it is not our job to save people. Jesus does the saving, and according to John 6:44, no one can come to Jesus unless the Father draws him or her. When I shared this teaching in our evangelism training all those years ago, it revolutionized our team. God gave me strict orders that were so new to my teams and me. He said, *Don't ask people if they are Christians. Don't ask them if they go to church. Just speak My words and lead them to Me.*

I was brought up in a church environment where we witnessed to people with tracts and had a prearranged set of questions to ask them. The Lord revealed to me that those methods were now ineffective. That was the old wineskin. The new methodology is Spirit-led evangelism. The gifts of the Holy Spirit must be front and center when ministering to the lost. Many people will not come to God unless He reveals the secrets of their hearts. Yet He wants to talk to people in this way, and He wants to use you and me to do it.

When my team and I began operating in prophetic evangelism, we saw many salvations, healings and miracles take place right there in everyday life. All we had to do was love people and release the words of the Lord to them. I have ministered to so many unbelievers in detailed prophetic words, and they always seem to ask, "How do you know this about me? Who told you this?"

Many of them stood with tears in their eyes as I told them, "These are the words from Jesus Christ to you. He loves you so much, and He wants a real relationship with you."

Wow, I am always amazed at how God still speaks today and reveals the hidden things in people's heart. The next great awakening is coming through prophetic evangelism.

### Signs, Wonders and Miracles

In the days ahead, signs, wonders and miracles will be the norm. They will become the usual environment of churches and believers everywhere. We will no longer hear of them in rare instances, but they will now spread like wildfire. Jesus said certain signs will follow those who believe. In Mark 16:17–18, He gave us five specific signs that we as His disciples would see:

1. *In My name will they cast out devils.* Deliverance ministry will increase over the coming months and years. People who have been possessed by demonic forces will be set free. We will see mass deliverance as families, groups of people and communities are

delivered from oppressive forces. Churches will once again place emphasis on casting out devils. This will be one of the signs.

2. *They will speak in new tongues.* Pentecost is coming back to the Church. Many people and ministries will have a renewed Pentecost experience. More teaching will focus on the gift of tongues again. It is through the gift of tongues that we access a heavenly language that God and angels understand. It is through this gift that your innermost being is refreshed and connected to the Source of all creation. Jude 1:20 reveals that when we pray in the Spirit, we build up our most holy faith. Faith is needed for salvation. Faith is needed for healing. Faith is needed for miracles. Our faith is built through praying in the Spirit.

3. *They will take up serpents.* Although God's protection and covering from harm is in place for His disciples, this phrase about taking up serpents seems to have more of an allegorical meaning. Jesus often used the term *snakes* in His teachings to refer to demons or devils. This term is symbolic of evil. In Luke 11:11, He says (paraphrasing) if your son asks you for a fish, would you give him a serpent? Jesus was using this verse to show the difference between a good father and a bad father. He later makes the point of the apostles addressing false teachings and releasing the teaching of the Holy Spirit. So metaphorically speaking, Mark 16:18 is about the apostles rooting out false teachings and replacing them with sound doctrine.

4. *If they drink any deadly thing, it will not hurt them.* Jesus was in essence saying that if you consume

anything fatal or deadly while on a God-sent mission, you will be protected. It will not kill you. This is the supernatural hedge that He places around His ministers of the Gospel. The powerful force of the Holy Spirit will be evident in the lives of those whom God has sent on Kingdom assignments. In the future, we will hear more and more instances of how the Lord supernaturally intervenes when believers should have died.

5. *They will lay hands on the sick, and they shall recover.* Healing belongs to the believer. Not only has God given us power for healing; He has also given His sons and daughters the gift of healing. We can transmit healing to others. The next revival will come with great waves of healing. Creative healing miracles will occur. We will see people healed from rare diseases and cancers. These things have already been occurring, but they will increase significantly as God is pouring out His Spirit in the earth like we have never seen. We have heard of great moves of healing in previous years. God is restoring back to the Body the power of the laying on of hands. This is an ancient gift that has been given to the Church to transmit the power of God. And not only will we see healings occur by the laying on of hands; we will come into a day where healing will even take place in waves over groups of people where no one has laid a hand on them but the Holy Spirit.

These signs shall follow those of us who believe. This means that we will not follow the signs, but the signs will follow us.

God spoke something else to me that completely rocked my world. He said, *In this season, you will be the sign.*

This is true not just for me, but for you. You will be the sign to the unbeliever that God is real! People will look at your life and the testimony through you and be drawn to the Lord Jesus Christ.

## YOUR PROPHETIC FORECAST

It is essential to discern when seasons are changing around you in the spirit realm. You can discern the change of a spiritual season by noticing the differences in the patterns of your life. Information, patterns and atmospheres control or govern seasons. A harvest season is marked by separation, which is the removal from those things that are detrimental to the harvest. It is also marked by gathering. Your posture in the midst of a harvest determines how much you gather. The supernatural harvest you will see in your life will be a harvest of souls (winning people to Christ) and a harvest of the long-awaited promises of God. It is vital, however, that you don't miss out on your harvest season. Here are four prophetic instructions to help you reap in due season:

1. Don't become weary while you are doing what God has called you to do (see Galatians 6:9). Weariness leads to burnout, which could leave you too weak to gather at harvest time. Refresh yourself by staying encouraged and staying in the Word of God.
2. Be available for God to use. God wants to use you as a vessel to reach others who are currently bound. If you are not emptied out of yourself and yielded to God, He can't fully utilize you to impact others.

3. Get ready to work. Harvesting requires much work. That is the reason why Matthew 9:37 says the harvest is plentiful, but the laborers are few. Many people are not willing to put in the work required to reap a harvest. So you must ask the Lord to give you the grace to work diligently for your harvest.

4. Whatever you sow, you will reap (see Galatians 6:7). Sow the right seeds. Seeds can be symbolic of the Word of God, words that you speak from your mouth, effort, financial support, resources and more. Whatever you plant, you will reap.

## PROPHETIC HOPE

The harvest is not just coming; it is already here—right now! In the coming days, you will see a family harvest and salvations. There is an anointing being released to win family members to Christ. You will see God break through some of the hardest cases. Addictions will be broken, demonic oppression will be destroyed and many people will experience massive freedom and deliverance. Some will have supernatural visitations as the Lord pours out His Spirit upon all flesh. Some will have God encounters in dreams, visions and visible manifestations that will bring them into true repentance and right relationship with the heavenly Father.

## 12

# Changing of the Guard

So the last will be first, and the first last. For many are called, but few chosen.

Matthew 20:16

My first international trip, which I took in my early twenties, was one of the most memorable. Back then, we were gathering for a prophetic summit that would be the beginning of many others in the nations. I was beyond excited! I had been doing itinerate ministry for several years by that time. I had started as a young teenager and had traveled and preached the Gospel throughout the United State at conferences, revivals, training events and other powerful gatherings. I had preached in small churches in rural areas in the middle of nowhere, and I had seen some of the most powerful miracles and prophetic ministry take place in those gatherings. I had also preached at large churches and events. God had allowed me to experience a wide variety of atmospheres, ranging from some of the most free-spirited charismatic churches to some of the strictest traditional settings. No matter the occasion, God's Word was the same. No matter the size of the crowd, the denomination or the type of event, God still found a way to show up and minister to people right where they were. I am convinced that He specializes in getting around our man-made agendas, which we sometimes call services. Whatever we are doing, in whatever way we are doing it, He still ministers directly to the people who need it.

I had been preaching throughout the United States, but I had not yet been abroad. When I got word about going along on this event, I knew it would be the beginning of much international travel for me. And I was right. This event was to take place in London, England, and I could not wait to get there. I rushed aboard an older American Airlines plane. There were no screens on the back of the seats for watching movies. For the entire seven-hour flight, I was thinking and praying. When I arrived, I quickly fell in love with the area. I met some of the most amazing people, some from Croydon, a large outer borough of South London, and some from other parts of the United Kingdom. It was a powerful event! After it was over, I would return many times to the U.K. to do ministry tours.

On this first trip, I preached at several Redeemed Christian Church of God churches, as well as nondenominational churches. What made this first trip even more special was all of the sight-seeing we had the opportunity to do. After one morning session, the team that had traveled with me from the United States rushed to Buckingham Palace. For people who live in that area, the palace has probably lost its charm. For me, it was breathtaking. We made it there just in time to see a spectacular ceremony. Tens of soldiers stood there in their full traditional, elaborate uniforms. They had red coats, scarlet tunics, artillery rifles and the tallest bear-skin hats. The headgear alone was like something out of a movie. Some soldiers were on horses, while others stood on the ground. Then they began to move in unison in the most precise and choreographed way. They were performing their ceremonial guard duties as the group of soldiers who had been protecting Buckingham Palace was being replaced by a new group of soldiers. We had stumbled on the "Changing of the Guard" ceremony.

While I was standing there, in the midst of all of the excitement and wonder, the Holy Spirit began to deal with me about how what I was watching was a picture of what we would see happen in the Body of Christ. I could hear Him saying in my spirit, *The guard is changing . . . the guard is changing . . .*

## The Last Will Be First

Just as I witnessed the "Changing of the Guard" in London all those years ago, there is a spiritual changing of the guard happening right now. We will see it continue in the years to come. God is reordering seats and systems. Many believers who have been on the front lines, battling valiantly, will be given rest and reprieve. This is not so much about natural age, because the old and the young will both usher in the new move of God together. This is about a shift that heaven is instituting in the earth.

Perhaps you are reading this, and you have been in the background, serving the Lord faithfully. Your time is coming where the Lord will pull you into the forefront of the area that you have been called in. You may experience a coming forth at your job, in your local church or even in your community. Coming to the forefront in any capacity is not about being seen. It is about God trusting you to be effective.

Matthew 20:16 says, "So the last will be first, and the first last. For many are called, but few chosen." The word *first* in this text is the Greek word *protos*. It means first or foremost in time, place or order. It comes from a root word that means in front of, above or before. Let's unpack those first three definitions: first in time, place or order.

### The Appointed Time

Because you have been called and chosen by God, you are about to step into His divine timing for your life. There have been prophetic words spoken over your life and promises in the Word of God that you have not seen manifest. It is not because you have done wrong or because something is out of place; sometimes it is because it has not been the time yet. I want to make this prophetic announcement to you: *The spiritual seasons are now changing, and it is your time. You will experience a due season, or an appointed period of time that God has created just for you to emerge in what He has called you to do.*

As we talked about in chapter 4, the Greek word *kairos* means "appointed time." I believe that God has appointed a time for you to excel, prosper and accomplish whatever He has for you. The time is now. If you receive this prophetic word, you will begin to see it manifest in your life. You may have been praying and asking God, *When do I step out and do what You've called me to? When should I launch that ministry? When should I write that book? When should I start that business?* For many believers, the time is now! You will be first in time.

### The Right Place

Timing is important, but placement is everything. It is possible for you to have all of the tools and resources you need to plant a garden. You have your seed and fertilizer, and you are ready to work. But if you are in the wrong field with the bad soil, nothing will grow.

You may have experienced this spiritually, where you were in a season where everything you needed was there—except the place. I experienced this for years. I lived in North Carolina and pastored a great ministry. I loved the area and had the opportunity to serve some of the best people, but the fullness of what God had put in me could not bloom there. I worked hard and prayed hard in that place, and by God's grace many lives were impacted, yet still there was no full manifestation of what God had promised. The Lord spoke to me that I was to move to Minnesota. He said to me, *I've given you the vison, but this is not the place.* When I obeyed Him and made that move, everything changed for the better.

Your situation may not be as drastic as mine was, and God does not always require a geographical move. Sometimes it is as simple as being in the right place spiritually. Having the right spiritual posture and mind-set can change everything. For you personally, the changing of the guard may manifest as a renewed mind and spiritual posture rather than a change of location. If you will yield to the leading of the Spirit, He will reorder your life and bring you into the right spiritual place.

### Rank and Order

So much rearranging is going on in the Spirit right now. Sometimes the Lord will allow your life to be completely turned upside down, so that He might put you into His proper order. Order deals with your position and rank. When the Bible says the first will be last and the last will be first, it is referring to order. When God reorders your life, if you have been faithful to His will, He will cause you to expand in your capacity. That deals with how much you can handle. He will also cause you to expand in your influence and your level of authority.

Matthew 25:14–29 tells the famous parable of the talents. The master of the house was traveling to a far country and left his servants in charge of his goods. To one he gave five talents, to another he gave two talents, and the last servant received one. Verse 15 explains that the master gave an the number of talents that he based on the skill level and ability of each servant. This is exactly what God does. He gives to us what we are able to handle at the time. Through a process of character maturation and development, He then adds to what we have.

In this parable, the servant who received five talents invested them and doubled what he had. The servant who received two talents did the same, doubling his investment. The servant with the one talent, however, dug a hole and buried it in the ground. The master was furious with this last servant because he did not manage well what he had. When something is managed well, by divine right it will multiply. The master said to him, in effect, "I'll take what you have and give it to someone else." But to the servants who managed what they had been given appropriately, he said, "Well done, good and faithful servant; you were faithful over a few things, I will make you ruler over many things" (verses 21, 23). He gave these two faithful servants an immediate rank and position change. Likewise, you have managed the little you have had well, and the Lord is giving you an immediate rank change in the Spirit.

## Leader Shifts

Over the past several decades, we have witnessed the transition of many of those who have stood guard spiritually as generals in the Body of Christ. We will see much more of this ahead. The Lord spoke this word to me that was very sobering: *In the next few years, you will see many of the pulpits change in America and the Church abroad.*

We are in the days of transition in every area of leadership, not just in the Church. A changing of the guard is happening in every sector of the world and its systems. Some leaders who have occupied key seats are now being relieved of their duties, as a new shift and order is coming into place. And for a space of time there will be many vacancies, as a new regime is being released. In fact, I saw this vision of shoes that were left in place, as though a person had been in them but there was no one there. There were many of these shoes in many empty rooms. The Lord said to me, *These are the vacancies left unoccupied in the Spirit. People must be raised up and equipped to fill them.*

New leaders will be raised up in this hour to fill these vacancies in the Spirit. Some of them are now living out in the field the way David did, just tending the sheep, but a giant warrior is awakening on the inside of them, just waiting to come forth.

 ## YOUR PROPHETIC FORECAST

You have the most amazing opportunity to be part of a great shift that is happening in the earth. Sometimes when people hear of the changing of the guard, they think of it in a negative light. But it is a necessary change. On a natural job, a shift change allows those who have been working to rest and those who have been resting and preparing to now work. You may be the very one whom God is raising up and preparing to fill a vacant seat in the spirit realm.

Along with this, when there is a changing of the guard, there is also a thrust to the forefront. It is possible that God is bringing you to the front in your career, family, community, church or ministry. Because of this, you must be prepared to handle the pressures of being on the front lines. Here are some takeaways to help you navigate coming to the forefront:

- Be faithful over what God has entrusted into your hands, no matter how small or insignificant it may seem. When you are faithful over a few things, the Lord will increase you to oversee many.
- Be prepared for criticism. Anytime God pushes you to the front in any area, you are going to be criticized and even judged for the decisions you make, because more of the spotlight is on you. Use that to your advantage, to uphold godly principles and be an example to others.
- The front line takes the first hit. In a battle, the front line must be prepared to take the brunt of the warfare. For this reason, you must clothe yourself in the armor of God, according to Ephesians 6:10–18.
- The last takeaway for you from this prophetic announcement of the changing of the guard is to pick up the mantle. When the Lord places the assignment, mandate or mantle on you, don't let the call pass you by. Seize the moment and walk fully in the assignment of God for your life!

 **PROPHETIC HOPE**

You are being brought to the forefront. Like David, you may have been in a cave or a hidden place, preparing for the next assignment or phase of life. But that season is coming to an end. As we continue to see the changing of the guard, the hand of the Lord is swiftly moving you to your rightful position and place in the Spirit. Some who have felt overlooked and unseen are coming into days of divine visibility. It is the plan of the Lord to bring you from the back to the front to carry out heaven's assignment for you in the earth.

# 13

# Political Upheaval

For nation shall rise against nation, and kingdom against
kingdom.

Matthew 24:7

I have had the privilege of traveling to more than 35 nations.
I have preached the Gospel throughout the United States, the
United Kingdom, Germany, the Middle East, Israel, multiple
countries in Africa and many other regions of the world. It
is only by the grace of God that I have found myself ministering everywhere from remote villages to large cathedrals.

This has all been exciting, but the most exciting experiences in ministry for me are when I am sent to a certain country just to minister to one person. I have seen some of the
greatest miracles and radical salvations happen as a result.
Over a decade ago, the Lord began to shift my ministry as a
governmental prophet, and He began sending me to minister detailed prophetic words to high-ranking governmental

leaders, ambassadors of nations, prime ministers and the like. God gets all the glory for opening these unique doors of ministry and for bringing His words to pass.

There is a huge difference between being called as a governmental prophet and being enmeshed and entangled with politics. Sometimes God may call us to intercede for certain countries or governments and even release specific words to them. Think about this: By effectively ministering to one high-ranking leader, you could be positively affecting hundreds of thousands, or even millions, of the people they govern.

In 2018, I was invited to minister in several nations. I went to about seven different countries on one trip. One of my main assignments was to minister to a group of people who work in high positions in the United Nations. When I arrived in Geneva, Switzerland, I began to pray with an urgency. I asked the people who were hosting me what they were bringing me in to do. They informed me that they wanted me to prophesy and pray in the United Nations' headquarters. God told me that He would shake up the U.N. and its dealings around the world. It was a powerful experience in Switzerland. Much prayer and prophetic ministry took place. As soon as I left one meeting, it hit headline news that the president of the United States had pulled out of the U.N. This was controversial and sent ripples throughout the world. The Lord allowed me to know through these that more political shakings were coming.

America has recently gone through a period of political division that is beyond anything we have seen in the past decade. The heart of the country has been more divided than ever, and the governmental landscape will only get worse. America and the nations of the world are stepping into an era of political upheaval.

The definition of *upheaval* is "a radical change, extreme agitation and disorder."[1] It denotes a violent disruption or change in a society or system. The etymology of the word comes from a Germanic root meaning "convulsions in a society." During this period of upheaval in politics and government, corruption and wickedness will be on display and be exposed. The Holy Spirit said to me, *Don't think it a strange thing when you see wicked legislation being substituted for godly, moral laws. You will not be able to legislate My words in some natural courts; they must be written upon the hearts of men.*

For too long, the Church has tried tirelessly to change legislation in the natural. Some of these efforts have proven successful, while in other areas they have failed. We must remember that our battle is in the court of heaven and not the courts of mankind.

## The Beginning of Sorrows

Matthew 24:7–8 states, "For nation will rise against nation, and kingdom against kingdom. And there will be famines, pestilences, and earthquakes in various places. All these are the beginning of sorrows." Jesus spoke of the times where sorrow would increase within the world. We are living in those times once again.

The beginning of sorrows points to the start of an intense period of tumult. Many in the prophetic community do not like to speak or prophesy these words, because they fear that such words are not encouraging. But these are the words of God. The Lord spoke this to me plainly as I was praying for the nation of America and this new era. He told me that the world has entered the beginning of sorrows. I had never studied this phrase, so I had no idea what it really meant.

As I carefully pursued God's heart about it, He began to unfold the meaning to me. In this new decade and beyond, we will see some of the greatest disasters that the earth has ever known. Political infighting and prolonged conflicts will be at an all-time high. Wickedness in high places will persist, and because of this, many will suffer the negative effects. But in the midst of it, God has a plan. And His plan will be in full effect.

The potency of this prophecy can be found in the word *sorrows*. In the Bible passage we just looked at, this is the Greek word *odin*. It means "intolerable anguish in reference to calamities." More importantly, the word means the pain of childbirth, travail and birth pangs. This speaks volumes! The governments of this world will be in a period of sorrows. This will involve the pangs of birthing. It will be the travail over the new thing that God will do.

In this upheaval, anguish and birthing, you will see some governments fail. And I saw in an unfolding vision that some European nations will see their governments be bankrupted and fractured. In the United States, the governmental fractures will begin to implode, but in the midst of it, new and fresh political voices will arise. This period of sorrows will give way to solutionists who will rise up to fix temporarily the ailments within the nation. Ultimately, however, it will be the Ekklesia, the Church, that rises to the occasion as the Body of Christ to speak peace into the governmental systems in the midst of massive calamity. I want to share with you a few specific prophetic words and visions God has given me about these coming times.

### Prophecy of a Third Party

Although it is said that the founding fathers of the United States did not intend or plan for partisan politics, in the 1790s the two-party system emerged. Since America's infancy, the country has been run by a two-party system that evolved into Republicans and Democrats. There are other smaller parties such as the Libertarian Party and the Green Party, but they don't carry the following, influence or political power of the two main political parties. God spoke this to me about the changing of the party structure in America:

> *Out of the chaos of the previous political season shall emerge the beginnings of a new political party. This party will be different from the others. For there is a people that have been crying out for change. They have been rejected and ousted from the establishment and status quo. Many will say that it will not happen, but yes it will emerge—a new party. A third party!*

I saw in a vision from God the major news media carrying this banner of a third party. It will shock the country and send ripple effects throughout the nations. It will trigger other countries to begin to formulate new party systems within their government. And the Lord added, *The voice of the people will cry, "We are done with the establishment!"*

We will see this prophecy come to pass. It will not, however, be the answer to America's political dilemma. It will only be the beginning of a new era in politics and government. The answer for the political mess that this country has found herself in is not a political party. The mess can only be fixed by Jesus Christ, the Light of the world, and by His Church arising to her place as the light of the world.

### Prophecy of a Woman Who Will Lead

God said to me that in the near future, America will see its first female president. Her rise to power will be controversial.

It will be surrounded by sudden and swift changes. Nonetheless, this will be groundbreaking and will be part of a plan for a new order in the world.

Although it is biblical for women to be in key roles of leadership, and although women have made great leaders, this specific rise to power will be carried out with a new world order agenda. In the Spirit, I saw an abrupt change come in the country as she stepped into her role of leadership. She has been secretly groomed for this position, and she will take the country into uncharted territories. She will lead as Commander in Chief at a time of national and international conflict and war.

### The Supreme Court Prophecy

The Lord took me into a vision in which I saw several faces change on the Supreme Court. This change will be marked by another time of transition and sudden death.

When I looked farther in this vision, I was unaware of how far ahead in time this change would be. Some of the words of the Lord that He reveals will happen in a matter of months, while with other visions or prophecies there is a sense that you have been carried many years ahead. I could not tell the timing of this one, but what I saw was very clear. I saw the seats on the Supreme Court expand. For the Lord says,

> *This will be groundbreaking in the history of America. The seats on the Supreme Court will be expanded, and more judges will be added. At the time, people will say, "How is it possible, or how could this happen?" Many will try to fight it, and some will even call it a coup and unconstitutional. Yet the expansion shall occur, and the face of the Supreme Court will be forever changed.*

### *Vision of the Battle over Gun Laws*

The epic battle over gun laws will rage on. Unfortunately, there are dark spirits that are currently taking advantage of this great divide, and they will continue to do so. I saw in the Spirit that violence and mass shootings will increase and come to a boiling point in America. In the Spirit, I saw a document being signed into law, and as I looked in the vision, I saw that the document involved major gun reform. The Holy Spirit said to me that this would be the most restrictive gun reform that we have ever seen in the history of this country. And I saw the law being put into place.

Please note that I am not sharing my opinion on this issue of gun laws. I am simply telling you what I saw in the vision. Surrounding this reform, chaos will ensue. In the vision there was even great physical conflict and clashing that arose. Many people will take their guns into the streets and into public buildings. They will stand in government buildings as a show of force, to signify that they are withstanding the restriction. The Holy Spirit said to me that this will be a dark period that will come in this nation's future, but that America will survive it.

## The Government of God

It is true that in this era, we will see crazy political disturbances the world over that have never been witnessed before. In spite of all these things, we as believers should never worry. Everything in this earth is temporal and fleeting. The only things that are eternal are God and His Word, as well as those of us who believe on Him because we are in Him. The government of God trumps all earthly governments.

We must make sure that our focus and mission do not become an effort to change government. As followers of Jesus Christ, we have been given a position that is far above parliaments, government houses and even principalities. We are seated in heavenly places spiritually with Christ Jesus, according to Ephesians 2:6, which says that God has "raised us up together, and made us sit together in the heavenly places in Christ Jesus."

So what is the government of God? His government is where He sovereignly reigns. Isaiah 9:6 says, "For unto us a Child is born, unto us a Son is given; and the government will be upon His shoulder. And His name will be called Wonderful, Counselor, Mighty God, Everlasting Father, Prince of Peace." The word *government* here is the Hebrew word *misrah*. It means "rule, dominion and government," and it comes from a root word meaning "to contend with." Yes, the governments of the nations ultimately rest on the Lord and His master plan, but this refers to a higher government—the government of God.

## Unlocking the Kingdom of God

Furthermore, the word *government* is akin to the word *kingdom*. The government of God is expressed through the concept of His Kingdom. Jesus references this Kingdom concept in several portions of New Testament Scripture. The only Gospel Jesus ever preached and commissioned the disciples to preach is the Gospel of the Kingdom. Luke 16:16 (AMP) says, "The Law and the [writings of the] Prophets were proclaimed until John; since then the gospel of the kingdom of God has been and continues to be preached, and everyone tries forcefully to go into it."

We see three main facets of God's government represented in Scripture: *the Kingdom of God, the Kingdom of heaven,* and simply *the Kingdom*. Jesus uses all three of these to convey His teachings. Let's look at each one in a little more detail.

### 1. The Kingdom of God

This phrase *the Kingdom of God* shows up in Scripture 68 times. The New Testament describes what this Kingdom of God is. Romans 14:17 reveals that it is not in meat or drink, but it is in righteousness, peace and joy in the Holy Spirit. These are keys of the Kingdom of God. To access this entity, we must use those keys. There is no other way.

Righteousness is to be in alignment with God and His will and purpose for your life. That can only be found through embracing a personal and real relationship with Jesus Christ.

Peace is a gift given to believers. When Jesus was preparing to go away to His Father in heaven, He told His disciples, "Peace I leave with you, My peace I give to you" (John 14:27). That word *peace* means a prosperity of the soul that spills over into one's life. It is purity and soundness of mind. Peace is needed to unlock the Kingdom of God.

Lastly, joy means gladness. It is akin to being happy and whole in God. This is a commodity that is needed to access the Kingdom of God. Without joy, peace and righteousness, the Kingdom of God is not fully manifested in a person's life.

So then, the Kingdom of God is His domain. When you allow Him to become the Lord of your life, then His Kingdom is reigning over you.

### 2. The Kingdom of Heaven

In order to understand *the Kingdom of heaven*, we have to understand the heavens and what they entail. In 2 Corinthians 12:2, Paul mentions being caught up in the third heaven. The Bible gives us the understanding that there are three heavens. As we talked about in chapter 3, the first heaven is the visible sky that we can see. The second heaven is what we would consider outer space, which is so vast that with all our technology and exploring, we still have not scratched the surface of it. The laws of the second heaven are different, and traversing it in our natural bodies is nearly impossible. Then there is the third heaven, which is where God resides.

The Kingdom of heaven is unlike the Kingdom of God, in that the Kingdom of heaven is the geographical location that houses the government of God. As Jesus preached the Gospel of the Kingdom, He made people aware of what was occurring spiritually. Matthew 4:17 says, "From that time Jesus began to preach and to say, 'Repent, for the kingdom of heaven is at hand.'" As Jesus walked the earth, He was declaring in this kind of statement that the Kingdom of heaven was colliding with earth. He was proclaiming that God's government was now superseding the government and kingdoms of man.

### 3. The Kingdom

There are points in the New Testament where the authors simply refer to *the Kingdom*. The three expressions *the Kingdom of God*, *the Kingdom of heaven* and *the Kingdom* are not to be confused as being the same thing. They have different meanings. James 2:5 says, "Has God not chosen the poor of this world to be rich in faith and heirs of the kingdom which He promised to those who love Him?" When the Bible uses the phrase *the Kingdom* in this way, it is a separate entity. This Kingdom is God's culture in the earth. God's culture includes our application of His customs and instructions for living, thinking and being. As believers, this Kingdom is our inheritance because we are servants and ambassadors of the King.

I explained God's government through these three facets to show you what you have access to, where you live spiritually and what you carry. Luke 17:21 (KJV) says, "Behold, the kingdom of God is within you." Wherever you go as a believer, you carry the Kingdom. You carry God's government, His domain and His culture in the earth. The political mess that the world is currently in, and that we will continue to see in the days ahead, will be disruptive and disastrous. In spite of it all, God is not shaken by what happens in the earth realm, and neither should we be. We are seated in heavenly places with Christ. We therefore occupy the government of God, and we legislate in the Spirit. When we pray, we access the courts of heaven, and the ultimate Judge releases His decree in the earth. And His decrees cannot be overturned!

##  YOUR PROPHETIC FORECAST

In the midst of political upheaval, you must disassociate from divisive and destructive politics that demonize others who think differently than you. We do know that the Word of God is our standard for living, but we don't make those who believe differently villains. We were sent to minister to and love them, not to make them enemies.

Although at times we must engage with politics, political parties should not be our go-to for solving social, economic or other problems that affect our countries. There has been a demonic assault against the Church to divide her over party lines and political issues. The Church is bigger than a political party or organization. In the coming months and years, major political conflicts and shakings will arise. In order to remain unscathed from the fray, this short list will help you navigate the road ahead:

1. *Guard and strengthen your heart*: Luke 21:26 (KJV) says we will see "men's hearts failing them for fear,

and for looking after those things which are coming on the earth: for the powers of heaven shall be shaken." Because of the major shakings in the high places (governments) of the earth, you must guard your heart. Fear is a dark spirit that will target humanity. You have the authority to dispel fear in the name of Jesus Christ and to pray for strength. Many will be in fear and anguish at what they see coming on the earth, but you will align with heaven and rise above the fear and see the salvation of the Lord.

2. *Remember that you are heaven's ambassador*: Because you are seated in heavenly places with Christ Jesus, you are His representative in the earth. You must remember that the government is upon His shoulders. Our battle is not with flesh and blood. The war is not with or against people. We are engaging with the spirits of darkness of this world. We are at war with principalities and ruling powers. These battles cannot be fought in the natural or even through political systems. They must be won in the heavens. And the good news is, the war has already been won.

3. *Laws will change*: Daniel 7:25 says, "He shall speak pompous words against the Most High, shall persecute the saints of the Most High, and shall intend to change times and law." It is the job of Satan, our adversary, to change laws so that they are against the will and heart of God. When you see these things, rest assured that no natural law can stop the Word of God. Your job is not necessarily to try to change or defend natural laws. As a believer, your responsibility is to hold fast to the Word of God in the midst of

changing times and laws. Be the light and share the love of Christ. Your mission is much more powerful than changing a law. As a Christian, you are in the business of changing and converting people's hearts.

4. *Intercession is the key*: No matter what you see going on around you, whether in government or another world system, your greatest weapon is prayer. Your communication with God must not be broken. I have been in several countries over the years that were plagued with political unrest. Through the agreement and unity of committed groups of intercessors, the Lord overthrew the demonic powers using and buffeting the governments of those nations. It is your intercession that will make crooked paths straight and release the angel armies of heaven to war on behalf of cities, regions and nations.

 **PROPHETIC HOPE**

You are part of the greatest entity on the face of this earth—the Church. The Church is God's governmental agency. As you speak the words and the Word of God, you will see peace manifest in the midst of chaos. You will see stability come where there is upheaval. As Christ's ambassador, when you pray and declare His Word, cities are changed, communities are impacted, nations are drawn to the Father and demonic agendas are annihilated. Remember your authority and the power that you have through Christ Jesus. You are His change agent in the world.

# 14

# Judgment in the House of God

For the time has come for judgment to begin at the house of God; and if it begins with us first, what will be the end of those who do not obey the gospel of God?

1 Peter 4:17

As we grow through life, we all face the challenge of learning obedience. Sometimes the very thing that we think we want could actually harm us. God is such a loving Father that He protects us even when we don't realize it. I started in ministry at a young age. My parents were pastors and taught me the ways of the Lord very early. I grew up in a very strict religious household, with very loving parents. Although I was passionate about the things of God and loved Him very much, my view toward God was distorted by my environment and by my own perception. I thank God to this day for the principles I learned as a child, but in my mind I magnified the strictness above the lovingness, and it affected how I saw

God. When I was ordained as a young minister, I remember being afraid of God punishing me for making any mistake. I did not realize it at the time, but embedded in my psyche was a view that God was this distant, angry Judge waiting to punish me for my mistakes. This caused me to do many things out of religious obligation and not relationship.

Years beyond that point in my life, God would take me on a journey of understanding true relationship with Him. I would learn that He is not this tyrant looking down and waiting to punish people for their wrongdoing. He is a loving Dad guiding and protecting His children. Every instruction in His Word is for our guidance and protection and is given to us so that we can live an abundant, enjoyable life in Him.

My warped view of God opened the door to a spirit of fear, superstition and anxiety. Due to rejection and brokenness, I could not receive His love. It was right there waiting for me to open up, but I did not know it. When God would correct me in an area, I saw it as punishment. Because of my own brokenness, my mind twisted judgment into wrath. Hebrews 12:6 says, "For whom the LORD loves He chastens, and scourges every son whom He receives." The Lord only disciplines, corrects and chastens those whom He loves.

It is true that when someone really loves you and sees you going down a destructive path, he or she will rebuke you to save your life. If God did not love you, then you would never experience His righteous judgment and correction in different areas. When God judges a situation or a person's heart, He is making a determination concerning that person's motive or action. If He sees you going off course, He will do everything short of violating your free will to bring you back into right alignment. Even if this hurts you temporarily, it will save you from eternal destruction.

God's judgment is not to be confused with punishment. The word *punishment* means "the infliction of a penalty as retribution for a wrongful deed."[1] This does not mean that there are not severe consequences for wrong actions; it means that Jesus took on our punishment on the cross. He provided the way for salvation and true repentance. With one act of repentance, you can be instantly restored!

## The Threshing Season

The word *judgment* in the Greek language is *krithinos*. It means "a decree or condemnation of a wrong decision." It comes from the root word *krino*, and it means "to separate, select, pick out or choose." It further means to resolve or determine—to judge. The word *judgment* in 1 Peter 4:17 sums up what it means for there to be judgment in the house of God. During this season of winnowing and threshing, God is separating those who are His and those who are not. This threshing season is necessary in the Body of Christ.

According to Matthew 13:30, the wheat and tares must grow up together. Tares are a type of weed that grows among grain, specifically wheat. When wheat and tares are growing, you cannot tell them apart. They look so similar that it would be detrimental to try to pull up the tares before they mature, because you would inevitably pull up wheat by mistake.

Jesus instructed that the wheat and the tares must grow together until the harvest. At harvest time, you can see fully the fruit that they bare. It is said that the tares develop black dots when they are fully mature, which makes them stand out strikingly from the wheat. Only at that time can the two be separated. This is a picture of God's judgment. It is

175

the separation between holy and unholy, clean and unclean, profane and sacred.

Jeremiah 5:31 says, "The prophets prophesy falsely, and the priests rule by their own power; and My people love to have it so. But what will you do in the end?" This represents three specific areas that God is cleansing. In this time of separation, He is cleansing His people, purifying His prophets and purging His priests. Let's look at each of these individually.

### God Is Cleansing His People

You may notice in your own life that God is requiring you to let go of some things and behavior patterns that are not beneficial to your walk with Christ. This is the first act of cleansing. It is decluttering the mind and soul. A person's soul is intricate and complex. It contains the human will, emotions and faculty of reason. The mind is embedded in the fibers of the soul. The human soul is sort of like a container. Throughout your journey in life, your soul will collect memories, impressions, desires, hopes and aspirations. You will store up fragments of time in the container of your soul.

Unfortunately, your soul will also collect hurts, painful memories, wounds, bruises and traumatic experiences. Some of these you may not even remember because they get shuffled down to the bottom of your container (soul). It only takes one jolt to your container, however, to send those forgotten fragments of time rushing to the surface. Attached to the fragments of time may be painful emotions that erupt through your personality and expressions. This can manifest as emotional torment, anguish or pain.

I find that many people are struggling through disfunction or disorder. A broken soul, undealt with, can pollute the heart and open the door to sin, rebellion and ungodly actions. For this reason, God is judging the areas of the heart that must be cleansed, corrected and healed. In Psalm 26:2 (NIV) David says, "Test me, LORD, and try me, examine my heart and my mind." This should be the cry of all of our hearts—*Search me, God! Examine my heart and mind to see if there is anything in me that's not like You!* When we pray this prayer, God will show us those things that are not like Him. And then we must allow Him to take them out.

### God Is Purifying His Prophets

Over the next several years, we will see waves of purification washing through God's prophets, prophetic circles and companies. Much refining and reformation will emerge during these times. God is judging prophets on their motives and how they have stewarded their prophetic offices. A standard is being raised once again, and the emphasis is on character above spiritual gifts.

There are those who have walked away from integrity, to prophesy only what the people want to hear. There are those who have prophesied based on political party affiliations and their own opinions and agendas. Then there are those who have prophesied for money or personal gain. These are all things that the Lord despises.

In order to protect the sanctity of the prophetic office, and most importantly, to protect His people, the Lord is releasing His refiner's fire. The purifying power of God will begin to sweep through prophetic camps. Many who have strayed will be restored because of their true repentance. Others who refuse to repent will be moved out of the way, to make room for an emergence of a pure prophetic breed of people who will begin to arise.

### *God Is Purging His Priests*

The priests in Jeremiah 5:31 are symbolic of today's Church leaders, the pastors. This verse says that the priests were ruling by their own authority—meaning that they were not submitted to God's will. One of the most dangerous weapons against the Church is a an unsubmitted or rebellious leader. Leaders are given the responsibility of serving the congregation. A higher level of influence is given to pastors and leaders. Because of this, those who teach the Word are judged more strictly, as James 3:1 proclaims: "My brethren, let not many of you become teachers, knowing that we shall receive a stricter judgment." There is a greater separation and pruning process for preachers and teachers of the Word.

In this upcoming season, pastors will be refreshed, purged and pruned for the new thing that God is instituting in the earth. It is going to take a new wineskin, remolded vessels of honor before the Lord. In the coming months, you will see many pastors in transition. Some will step down from large megachurch congregations because their spiritual time of serving in that capacity is over. Some leaders will transition in other ways. When you see these things, you will know that God is realigning His priests.

Globally, the Church has entered into the days of judgment in the house of God. The Body of Christ has begun a period of cleansing. God is purging and cleansing His house in order to prepare His Bride. This cleansing is necessary in order to align the Body with her original call and purpose.

## The Spirit of Another Jesus

It has been sad to witness the corruption and demonic infiltration among those who have called themselves the house of God. There was a day where the fear of God dwelt within His people, and we walked circumspectly before the Lord. There was a time when people were much more open to the spirit of conviction for sin and wrongdoing. Now we have seen the rise of a brazen people who have lost the fear of the Lord. Many disrespect God's altar and sacred house with profane behavior and blasphemous doctrine. Over the past several years, there has been the deceptive propagation of false teachings, which have now become so intertwined with popular preachers and personalities that people cannot tell the difference between the truth and a lie.

An evil spirit is lurking within the corridors of the Church, inside the four walls of this institution. It masquerades itself under a costume called *religion*. The religious spirit is one of the greatest enemies of the true Church of Jesus Christ. False religion simply places constraints on people by telling them what they cannot do and by putting them in the prison of earning approval from the doctrines of man. This evil spirit takes the Word of God and twists it for its own benefit and advancement. This spirit rejects the truth of God's Word and embraces a lie. It teaches its followers the blessing principles of the Bible without the character of Christ. This false beast, coupled with false religion, is *the spirit of another Jesus*.

The apostle Paul wrote of this in his epistle to the Church in Corinth. He warns in 2 Corinthians 11:4, "For if he who comes preaches another Jesus whom we have not preached, or if you receive a different spirit which you have not received, or a different gospel which you have not accepted—you may well put up with it!" Another Jesus. This is a scary picture, that it is possible that anyone in the household of faith would receive the spirit of another Jesus. Sadly, this spirit is already rampant in the Church, and in the coming days we will see it rear its head even more. Here are some characteristics by which we can identify this false spirit:

- *Painting Jesus as the champion of any political party.* The true Jesus Christ of the Bible did not get entangled with earthly political systems. During Jesus' days on earth, the Jews were awaiting a Messiah who would overthrow the Roman government and set them free from that oppressive system. Jesus informed them that He had already overcome the world (see John 16:33).

- *Portraying Jesus as a supporter of any lifestyle.* This false spirit will insist that if you love everyone, you can live any way you want to live, and God is okay with it. The true Jesus Christ of the Bible loves everyone, but He does not support just living any way you feel like living. This is why, after He spared the woman's life when she was caught in adultery, He said to her, "Go, and sin no more" (John 8:11). Jesus does not condone sin, but He also does not condemn the world because of it. He is right there with His arms outstretched, offering freedom and salvation.

- *Creating the narrative that Jesus was just another prophet.* The spirit of another Jesus says that He was just another prophet, like Muhammad or like any of the other wise, religious leaders throughout history. This could not be further from the truth. The Jesus Christ of the Bible is the Messiah and Savior of His people and of the world. He is called the Messiah in Matthew 1:1.

- *Purporting that Jesus is only a way of life.* This spirit of another Jesus says that He is only one of many ways to get to the heavenly Father. It teaches that there are multiple ways people can get to know God. This is a lie! In John 14:6 Jesus exclaimed, "I am the way, the truth, and the life. No one comes to the Father except through Me."

We must be careful of this false spirit of another Jesus that has crept into the Church and is rampant in the social sectors of society. We must hold onto the pure teachings, principles and character of Jesus Christ shown in the Holy Scriptures. And even more so, we must have a personal relationship with our Savior, which allows us to be transformed into His image. Because there has been a diluting of the Gospel in some circles, the Lord is bringing a separation between those who are His and those who are not. There will be a separation between those who believe in the true Gospel and those who believe in a cheap copy. For this reason, God is shaking His house, and we will see the judgment of God begin.

## YOUR PROPHETIC FORECAST

"For if we would judge ourselves, we would not be judged," says 1 Corinthians 11:31. The Amplified translation says, "But if we evaluated and judged ourselves honestly [recognizing our shortcomings and correcting our behavior], we would not be judged." Although many people look at judgment as a bad thing, it has been ordained by God. According to the apostle Paul, we are instructed to judge ourselves. This is a powerful verse of Scripture that I endeavor to live by. If you evaluate and examine yourself, you will not have to be judged or examined by others. In other words, God gives you and me the ability to self-correct.

181

Correction is life, safety and security for the future. Correction is a gift from God designed to keep us from self-destruction. If you adjust your mind-set to see correction as a gift, you will posture yourself for success in every area of your life. Below, I have created a self-evaluation checklist to help you judge yourself and align with God's purpose for your life.

### Self-Evaluation Checklist

1. What is my motive for what I am doing?
2. Am I serving as unto the Lord, or for personal gratification?
3. Am I helping in order to be seen, or out of love?
4. What is the condition of my heart toward others?
5. Am I holding unforgiveness toward someone?
6. Have I been hurt or wounded recently, or in the past?
7. Have I healed from that past hurt or recent wound?
8. Am I living in a pattern of sin? If so, how can I lay those things aside to align with God's will?
9. Do I need to repent of wrongdoing?
10. Am I hiding things from God or from people in my life?
11. Do I need to disconnect from people who have a negative influence?
12. Have I opened the door to demonic influence by violating God's Word?
13. Am I open to God's cleansing power in my life?
14. Am I open to God's correction in my life?

This is just a simple evaluation to get you started on searching, investigating and self-correcting. It will start you on a path of transparency and honesty with yourself and with the Lord. It is a wise person who desires to know what is in his or her own heart. As God reveals what may be hidden in you, repent and immediately allow Him to cleanse your heart and mind.

## PROPHETIC HOPE

According to Hebrews 12:6, "whom the Lord loves He chastens." Correction is a sign that God loves you so much that He wants you to succeed. After a season of judgment or correction comes growth, rest, peace and the overwhelming joy and love of God. Even during a season of correction, you will be engulfed and surrounded by God's love. As you go through periods of realignment with the Lord, be encouraged and receive God's outpouring of mercy, grace and never-ending compassion toward you.

15

# The Hybrid Church

And every day, in the temple and from house to house, they
did not cease teaching and preaching that the Christ is Jesus.

Acts 5:42 ESV

Throughout the ages, the message of the Gospel has not
changed. It remains indestructible. We still hold so tightly
today to the core values Jesus presented in Scripture. The
attributes, character and teachings of Jesus Christ are invalu-
able at the core of our Christian faith. The methods, style
and institution of them, however, have changed over time and
through many phases of transition. If you are part of the
Church at large, it should be crystal clear that the Church
as we know it is in transition again.

Several years ago, as I was seeking God for His direction
for the church I pastor in Minnesota, He downloaded a set
of instructions to my spirit. He began dealing with me about
the need for our homes to become meeting places with the

Holy Spirit. I thought to myself, *Lord, I pray at my home and study the Word.* Yet I could sense that what He wanted was more intentional and strategic. God then gave me the assignment to begin reenergizing small group ministries in our church, groups that would take people's experience with the Word of God outside of the regular Sunday message. The first time I instituted this, it reinvigorated my church. People could experience the power of being connected in real fellowship with their brothers and sisters in Christ. The small groups went beyond a church service and brought ministry to real life.

When the pandemic of 2020 came in and large gatherings were banned for more than a year, I understood that God had been trying to prepare me to mobilize our church to be deployed outside of a Sunday service experience. Small group gatherings were the foundation of the early Church. The Church of the Lord Jesus Christ was not started in a cathedral, huge sanctuary or mega building, although those facilities are useful. The Church was birthed in outdoor gatherings, homes, caves and dens. And we will see a return to the book of Acts Church. This does not take away from the importance of organized ministry and the proper protocols that come with facilitating the local church. But it is part of what the future holds.

### Revival in Your House

The next major revival will start from the Church and spread into houses. God wants to set up a habitation in homes all over the world. In Genesis 2, after God masterfully created the heavens and earth, He wanted communion and fellowship, so He created Adam and subsequently the family unit. The family unit was the first Church, or "called-out ones." It was always God's intention for the family to be the nucleus, and from that entity everything else would be built. This is why Satan's greatest attack has been against the family. Through fractures, trauma and deceit, he has cunningly entered into homes so he can tear apart families. The result has been great conflict between mothers and daughters, and sons and fathers have been set at odds. This is a diabolical design of the enemy.

In this new era will come an even greater assault against the family unit, an assault unparalleled to anything we have seen. The enemy will attempt to further pervert the biblical family that God instituted. Although we will see this attack continue, at the same time houses of revival will be raised up. Many who have been praying will see their families restored back to God. Prodigal sons and daughters will return. Fractures and family wounds will be healed.

I see a wave of healing coming to families all over this nation. The spirit of Elijah is coming over your home. You will see God turn the hearts of the sons to the fathers and the hearts of the fathers to the sons. This signifies a generational unity and healing. The great divide is being mended.

What does revival look like in your house? Revival is always ushered in by passionate prayer and intercession. Your house will become a house of prayer. Spontaneous and divinely appointed prayer will erupt in your home. Sometimes this will occur with just one person, sometimes with friends or in a family gathering. Prayer is the vehicle that carries the movement of the Spirit. Houses will become altars where people will repent and come to Christ.

It is one of the best feelings to see people getting saved, set free and delivered right there in your home. This was the norm in my family house growing up. Prayer would be going on any time of the day and sometimes during the night. Guests would come and receive ministry. People were fed naturally and spiritually, and we shared fellowship. Growing up, it seemed to me as if we would take in almost anyone. As a kid, I witnessed devils being cast out from people who had been bound. They were set free right in our living room.

God was showing me through my early experiences that it is not so much just about your natural house; it is about allowing the Holy Spirit to move anywhere at any time, as He desires. I realized that God is not interested in filling buildings as much as He is interested in filling hearts. The next wave of revival will be about changing, transforming and filling hearts. The apostle Paul reminds us that God wants to dwell in our hearts: "Do you not know that your body is a temple of the Holy Spirit who is in you, whom you have from God, and you are not your own?" (1 Corinthians 6:19). Because the Holy Spirit dwells within you, you are carrying the move of God on the inside. Wherever you go is where there is an opportunity to unleash and release God's indwelling presence in your external environment.

**Revival in the Streets**

Decade after decade in Christian history, we have seen this search and quest for revival. Reports start buzzing that revival is breaking out over there or over here. Some say it is happening in California; others say it is happening in Florida. Now, don't misunderstand what I am conveying. Yes, revival does hover over cities and regions, but God's desire is to pour out His Spirit on all flesh, everywhere.

I was part of hosting the revival that broke out in Minneapolis after the killing of George Floyd in 2020 that sent ripple effects throughout the world. When the chaos ensued, my heart was to help as many people as possible who were suffering and who could not get food from stores because the stores had all been burned in that part of Minneapolis. The church that I pastor jumped into action. We began buying food from the suburbs and bringing it to ground zero of the chaos. People lined up for hours to receive the free food. Then something miraculous happened. Because the people's natural needs were being met, they became open to ministry. I had teams out praying for people and ministering to them spiritually. We saw many people give their hearts to the Lord, right there on the streets and in the parking lots. Other people who had drifted from God came back to the Lord. Obviously, we were excited to witness this!

Of course, the news media was buzzing because of all the chaos in the city. Then we shifted our ministry to the exact street where George had been killed. I started preaching on that street, along with other pastors and leaders. Many churches left their buildings and came out every day to pray, worship in the open air and minister to people. On one of the days when I was preaching on the streets, I saw healing erupt without anybody laying hands on anyone. God was certainly there as people screamed that they had just been healed of ailments they had suffered for years.

Major news outlets from around the country began contacting my ministry and me. Every day, they were calling for interviews. At first, I was totally against answering them. Then I heard the Lord give me the release to utilize the media to spread the Good News. Reporters began asking, "What is revival?" I would explain it to them, and then they would say, "We heard that people got healed. What does that mean, and how did that happen?" So, I started explaining to reporters about the healing power of God.

One day while I was on my way to minister on the street at the George Floyd site, I got a call from one of the organizers of the events there. He said, "We are going to move you to another day to preach." He informed me that a well-known music group was coming, and they wanted to change the schedule.

I didn't mind. I told him, "I'm coming anyway. I don't have to be on the stage; I'll just worship on the street."

I learned early on that God does not need a stage or man's pulpit; all He needs is a willing vessel. As I stood worshiping while the singers were singing onstage, the Holy Spirit told me to go stand in front of the portable baptismal pool that was set up at the site. It had been put into place, but it was not being used. I was told that George Floyd's family had permitted the baptismal pool at the site because at one time in his life he used to baptize people. While I was standing there, someone got saved right there in the crowd and said, "I want to be baptized." It was unplanned, unorganized and totally spontaneous. At that time, no one was really prepared for it. But because I was standing there, one of the organizers asked if I would baptize the person. I said yes and immediately jumped into the pool.

One after the other, people started getting saved, making a decision for Christ and being baptized. It was one of the most beautiful things I have ever seen. All of it was spontaneous. I was baptizing people and prophesying to them on the street for hours that day. It was powerful! So powerful that one of the news media people came up and said to me with teary eyes, "I've been trying to stay unbiased. But I can't anymore. I want to be baptized!" That day, the Lord refueled a passion for revival in me. The Church has been designed by God to house and host the spirit of revival everywhere.

## The Hybrid Church Model

One of the most detrimental things to the world is when the Church stays in the building. The book of Acts Church was a hybrid. Not only did the early believers have large gatherings and times of worship and the Word; they also worshiped, praised and shared the Word in every sector of society. The writer of Hebrews describes a people of faith throughout the ages who lived in the most uncomfortable situations yet kept their faith. Hebrews 11:38 (NIV) says, "The world was not worthy of them. They wandered in deserts and mountains, living in caves and in holes in the ground." Sometimes these believers lived in caves or dens or wherever they could, but because they were the *Ekklesia* (Greek), the Church prevailed.

Today, our caves, dens and deserts are the world systems in which we live. They are wherever we gather for work, living and engaging in society. The Church in the twenty-first century must adjust to the changing modes and platforms in which we now operate. In this era, virtual church services, gatherings and conferences will dominate. In-person gatherings are not going anywhere, but both types of gatherings will operate as converging systems. The religious systems will fight against these emerging virtual platforms, but they will not be able to stop them. God has ordained these changing platforms to propagate the Gospel in every corner of the world.

The world as we know it is changing. As a matter of fact, it has already changed. What we will see in the decades to come are the aftereffects of the change that has already occurred. Because the world has changed, the Church must adjust its sails to accommodate the changing wind. No, we are not compromising our principles, standards or faith.

We are simply adjusting our sails. The face of the Church is now being reordered to reach a generation that has rejected the Church and the ways of Christ. The new move that God is bringing in the Church will ruffle feathers, astound the religious and shake us to our core. But we cannot reject His move, just because we are uncomfortable. The Church will prevail, with even greater power in the days to come.

What does this hybrid model of the Church look like? It is the Church invading coffeehouses, social media platforms, the marketplace, corporate companies and more. God will use those who are willing to demonstrate the Kingdom wherever they are. Ministry will take place anywhere from the highest levels of government to the breakroom on your job. This is what the hybrid model looks like. Although we see some of this now, it is about to explode. The Word of God will be everywhere. We will see Christian virtual gatherings connect people from all over the world and break records. Millions of people will hear the Word at one time and worship the Lord together. The Church will partner with technology to bring in the next harvest. If you are uncomfortable with technology, you must familiarize yourself with it, because it is one of the main vehicles for the next move of God.

Because of this hybrid Church model, in-person worship will be so much more appreciated and valued. As believers gather in the same building in one accord, the power of God will erupt. Many in-person gatherings will explode, and houses of worship will grow. Some churches will hold services in the most uncommon places, but do not criticize them. The Lord will use them to reach a different crowd of people. From outdoor meetings, to malls, to schools, to movie theaters, God's Church will rise like yeast and make her impact.

YOUR PROPHETIC FORECAST

Having church and experiencing God in houses, on the job and in the marketplace will become the norm. This will be a necessity because of the chaos that will ensue in the world. The gathering of congregations in sanctuaries will, of course, remain. In the new era, however, the Church will be hybrid. With all the changes that are occurring and will occur over the next several years in the Body of Christ, it can be easy to feel uncomfortable or to feel that things are changing too quickly. Maybe you have been used to your church experience or ministry world looking the same for the past ten or twenty years. It is important that you understand that the change that is now occurring is of God. Knowing this will cause you to embrace what the Spirit is doing.

In addition, unconventional churches will emerge in the most unusual places, but they will reach a people who would not come into a church building. The most important point that you can understand regarding this subject is that *you are the Church*. And God is sending you into every area of society to demonstrate His love and His Word to those you encounter. God's people will expand rapidly on virtual platforms, with online services, revivals, panels, talk shows and podcasts that will reach people outside the institution of the Church.

It is also paramount that you ask the Holy Spirit how He wants to use you in this vital time to be the Church and to demonstrate His Word beyond what we know traditionally as church. Here are some questions you can ask yourself and take with you into your time of personal prayer:

1. How does God want to use me to help advance the Kingdom?

2. How does God desire to use me outside the four walls of the Church?

3. What kinds of people am I drawn to minister to?

4. Am I called to marketplace ministry?

5. What spiritual gifts do I have?

6. Am I resisting or embracing changes in the personal world of ministry? If I am resisting, how can I change that?

## PROPHETIC HOPE

Revival is here, and you are being positioned to be part of the next great move of God. As you avail yourself to God, He will use you in uncommon and supernatural ways to advance His Kingdom in the earth. You are carrying the glory of the Lord into your neighborhood, job and community. Your light will shine beyond the four walls of the Church and into every area of your life. You will find in the coming days that your greatest impact will be on those whom you encounter in your everyday life, whether at grocery stores, in restaurants or the like. The light of God in you will shine the brightest in the darkest of places.

16

# The Underground Church

They were . . . (people of whom the world was not worthy),
wandering in deserts and mountains and [living in] caves and
holes in the ground.

Hebrews 11:37–38 AMP

In the past several decades, the phrase *underground Church* has become commonly used in reference to groups of believers who operate in oppressive, communist countries all over the world. It was first used in the 1950s in connection with Chinese Catholic churches that refused to associate with the state-sanctioned, government-run church organization in the People's Republic of China. The underground Protestant churches of that time and place were generally referred to as *house churches*.[1] Since then, however, the term *underground Church* has spread beyond the Catholic Church, to include Protestant and charismatic churches alike that remain under oppressive governments that do not allow them to worship freely. Underground networks and house churches have sprung up throughout the oppressed nations.

The Middle East has seen its fair share of oppression against Christians. Over the years, there has been a rise in assaults against these kindhearted believers from their own governments. I have had the privilege of frequenting the Middle East, as well as other areas and countries while they were in the middle of crises. A few years ago, I was asked to preach in a country that was killing and beheading Christians. It was devastating to hear these reports. It was even more pressure-filled to be in the area at that time. I went anyway, with faith in the protection of God. I preached and saw the power of God move on those amazing people.

Later, I was asked to come and meet with a pastor of an underground church, to help strengthen him. My first thought from a natural, human perspective was, *What could I possibly do to strengthen this pastor?* I had been sitting in the comfort of the American Church environment for decades, with our plush seats and beautiful buildings, our nicely timed services and our pretty worship services. How do you identify with those believers who walk miles to get to a church service, when some of us have been living right down the street from a church and have just decided not to go? How do you understand the plight of believers who could be imprisoned for carrying a Bible or preaching the Gospel to the lost? Or even worse, many of them could be killed for evangelizing or professing the name of Christ. This experience caused me to reevaluate my own faith and walk with the Lord. I, too, had gotten use to the comforts and the lethargy of a commercialized church experience. When I met with this pastor, even though I was praying for him, I was the one who was strengthened more than I realized. The Lord used this experience to shake me to my core.

I began traveling to developing countries and persecuted areas to minister to the most amazing people, at times at the risk of my own safety. I have been held at gunpoint by Muslim guards and questioned by authorities about my Christian name, Joshua. Through these experiences, the Lord has placed a deeper passion in me and a deeper love for Him. It was through these experiences that God developed a deep hunger in me for Him, and a hunger to break the mold of mediocre, average Christianity and step into an authentic Christian faith. What an honor to be part of God's Body on the earth and to suffer for the sake of Christ.

You may be reading this and thinking, *But I've never been to China or the Middle East, or to the parts of Africa where Christians are jailed or killed.* Maybe you have never experienced the pressures of living under a government that is antagonistic toward your Christian faith. You don't have to have had those experiences, however, to suffer for the sake of Christ or to be part of an underground network. You get the opportunity to stand for Christ right there in your town. You get to represent Him well in your neighborhood, your local grocery store, your job or even your school.

You, too, can break the mold of mediocrity and be bold for Jesus Christ. You can raise the level of your hunger and passion for God by simply making a decision to seek Him and love Him with all of your heart. When you do this, you will encounter the Holy Spirit in the most unique ways. Then you must remember that you are part of a larger Body of believers all over the world. Even with our diverse experiences, expressions and sufferings, we are one.

## Prophecy of a Coming Persecution

There is a persecution coming to the Church in America and in other developed nations such as we have never seen in modern times. As Christians, we must prepare ourselves for the seasons of trouble, turbulence and conflict ahead. This is not a pretty message, and I understand that to some it will be controversial. But the Holy Spirit spoke this word to me so clearly: *Tell My people that persecution is coming. Persecution is coming to the Church in America, but My people aren't ready.* He went on, *The fivefold leaders must prepare and equip them for what is ahead. You must prepare them.*

This word shook me to my core. The Holy Spirit spoke it to me with such urgency. God does not always speak to me this way, but when He does, I stand at attention. This word caused me to seek Him for how to prepare and how to know what is ahead. Along with the challenges, He also showed me some of the benefits that come from facing persecution, which I will share in the "Your Prophetic Forecast" section at the end of this chapter.

In the coming years, we will see the rise of government-controlled churches in several nations. Many of them won't call themselves by that term, and you won't even know that is what is happening. In the Spirit, I saw secret organizations forming as branches of government in an effort to control the Church and the Church's impact and response in certain times of crises. This is a diabolical plot to shut down the voice of God's Church. This is the rise of an antichrist spirit that is already here in the world. And over the next few decades will come the greatest fight of the modern-day *Ekklesia*. People will say that the underground Church is no longer just in China or in some far-reaching part of the

197

world; underground networks will rise up all over to resist the spirit of the age that is raging.

In a vision from God, I saw a major push coming—yes, even in America—for the people and the culture to resist portions of the Bible that don't fit the agenda of the day. I saw the headline on a news outlet saying *Banned*. I was shocked to see this vision where certain verses and chapters of the Bible were prohibited and were even considered hate speech. This is a diabolical plot of the enemy to twist the Word of God to make it into something it is not. The Bible is a compilation of instructions from a loving Father to His children. If we heed the Word, we will find life. Despite what I was seeing in this vision, I also saw the Church push back with a massive wave of love without compromise.

## The Gates of Hell Will Not Prevail

Sometimes it can be quite daunting to hear of some of the things coming on the earth. Prophecies or visions of warning can be unnerving, to say the least. As a prophet, I have had to live with the blessing and the burden of seeing the future. When I was given a prophetic word in 2015 to prepare for 2020 and the new era that we would enter, I was a little shocked at what I heard and saw. At that time, the Lord spoke to me of a virus that would mimic other diseases, and I saw it in a lab in a vision. God said that it would be a strain we had never seen. I shared this with my church that year in a prophetic service, and many of the members recorded the prophecy. Then in 2019, the Lord showed me in a vision people wearing masks. In this vision, people in airports and all kinds of places had masks on. I was stunned because there was no talk of a pandemic at that time. The Lord warns us of things to come, however, that we might not be caught off guard.

Through the years, I have learned that when God speaks it or shows it, we need to respond by praying about it and preparing. There is no spirit of fear in the perfect love of God. The prophetic gifts are an expression of the love of God. Therefore, we must not panic about what we hear concerning the things that are to come. It is the massive love and compassion of God to share them with us and prepare us for them. Regardless of the evil forces that are operating in the world and those forces that will arise in the future, we have hope. God has designed and fashioned the light to diffuse the darkness. That's right—light is more powerful than darkness, even on your worst day!

We as God's people must be reminded that we are the light of the world, as Matthew 5:14–16 proclaims. Yes, we the Church carry this light that cannot be diminished. We are the Bride of Christ, and we will prevail. The Church will prevail through tumultuous storms. The Church will prevail through persecution. The Church will prevail through attacks and scandal. The Church will prevail through corrupt government and wickedness in high places. The Church will prevail through devastation and tragedy in the earth. Yes, the Church will prevail against the antichrist spirit and the spirit of the age that war voraciously against us. The Church has always prevailed, and it will continue to prevail.

So much hope is embedded in this one Scripture that Jesus shared: "And I tell you, you are Peter, and on this rock I will build my church, and the gates of hell shall not prevail against it" (Matthew 16:18 ESV). The word *prevail* in this text means "to overpower." God will not allow hell and its forces to defeat or overcome the Church. During days of persecution and darkness, we will see the Church overcome. And because you are part of the Church, God is giving you prevailing power—the power to withstand against evil.

Prevailing power is the ability to outmaneuver and outwit the wiles or strategies of the devil. No matter what we face in the coming years, God will cause us to triumph.

## YOUR PROPHETIC FORECAST

Persecution against the Church is inevitable. God has fore-warned us through the Bible, as well as through prophecy, that it is coming. You will be persecuted if you live for Christ. There is no way of escaping it, as 2 Timothy 3:12 makes very clear: "Yes, and all who desire to live godly in Christ Jesus will suffer persecution." Through the transforming grace of the Lord Jesus Christ on the lives of His people, we have been designed to withstand and abound amid adversarial environments. As I mentioned earlier, what it says in God's Word is true—that the gates of hell shall not prevail against the Church.

The more pressure that is placed on you as a believer, the more you will be transformed into the likeness of Christ. As difficult as it may be for some to believe this, there are massive benefits to suffering for His sake. God will repay you for all you endure for the Gospel. The following benefits of persecution will help you to focus on the outcome and not on your situation:

- Suffering brings about greater glory. "For our light affliction, which is but for a moment, is working for us a far more exceeding and eternal weight of glory" (2 Corinthians 4:17).
- Persecution unlocks a deeper depth of revival, with signs, wonders and miracles (see Acts 5:12–25).

200

- Suffering is training to reign with God. "If we endure, we shall also reign with Him. If we deny Him, He also will deny us" (2 Timothy 2:12).
- Affliction and persecution are tools for learning that produce godly character. "It is good for me that I have been afflicted, that I may learn Your statutes" (Psalm 119:71).
- Suffering is how we learn obedience to the will of the Father. "Though He [Jesus Christ] was a Son, yet He learned obedience by the things which He suffered" (Hebrews 5:8).
- From persecution, you will be rescued! As Paul said in 2 Timothy 3:11–12, "What persecutions I [Paul] endured. And out of them all the Lord delivered me. Yes, and all who desire to live godly in Christ Jesus will suffer persecution."

## PROPHETIC HOPE

Your declaration of hope in the midst of persecution is found in Isaiah 54:17, where God tells us, "No weapon formed against you shall prosper, and every tongue which rises against you in judgment you shall condemn. This is the heritage of the servants of the LORD, and their righteousness is from Me." Every agenda of the enemy will fail against your life. And no matter the affliction that you find yourself in, the Lord has promised to deliver you out of it—every time! Or reward you greatly in eternity for enduring until the end. You have already won through Jesus Christ, and you have the victory in every situation and trial.

# 17

# Merging of the Streams

*. . . until we all reach unity in the faith and in the knowledge of the Son of God and become mature, attaining to the whole measure of the fullness of Christ.*

Ephesians 4:13 NIV

Genesis 2:10 (AMP) speaks of a river that flowed from the Garden of Eden: "Now a river flowed out of Eden to water the garden; and from there it divided and became four [branching] rivers." If you could close your eyes and imagine the most beautiful, lush and vivid tropical oasis, I am sure you would pull up all sorts of amazing imagery. And just think, the Garden of Eden would probably be more beautiful still than what you imagined. Genesis 2 describes for us how the river's flow was designed specifically to water the Garden. In those days, there was no rain. Water came up from the ground, and through an unlimited network of rivers it brought refreshing to the Garden.

It is also interesting to note that when God created human-kind, He did not place the first family in a city; He placed them in a garden. Perhaps this is because everything in God's creation functions on a system of sowing and reaping. What better way for humankind to see that system demonstrated than in a Garden? Although Adam did not have to plow fields before his fall, surely he saw the trees produce in their cycles. I believe he learned about the power of a seed and the process of growth from his observations.

Likewise, within the Kingdom of God, everything runs on a system of sowing and reaping. If you sow negative and destructive words, you will reap negativity and destruction back as a harvest. If you sow and speak the words of God, you will see them come back to you and you will reap a harvest of bountiful blessings. The harvest is a huge part of the cycle of sowing and reaping, but it cannot take place without the proper watering system. The river in Eden was the Garden's irrigation system.

Today, varying rivers or streams are flowing in the spiritual that create movement in the Body of Christ. The term *stream* here is symbolic of a movement or company of people. In the Church world, this may be symbolic of groups of people who operate similarly or have comparable functions in the Church. Oftentimes, people of the same stream will pray, preach or even flow in the gifts of the Spirit in the same man-ner. It is like being part of a tribe. Everyone in a particular stream understands the same language and has similar ways of thinking when it comes to the things of God. There are prophetic streams, evangelistic streams, healing streams and so forth. Sometimes certain streams can be aligned with cer-tain denominations or organizational preferences.

Whether in the natural or in the spiritual, a stream can be a beautiful thing, yet it begins to diminish, decrease and decline when it does not meet up with a larger body of water. There are many streams of people in the Body of Christ who have been wondering where they have erred and why they have missed the mark, whether in prophetic perception or in gaining an understanding of what God is doing now. This has happened simply because their streams have been isolated far too long, so the flow has begun to wane. In the Garden of Eden, one river went out and became four heads. The source of the separate streams was the one original river. This is prophetic symbolism for today. The source of our spiritual streams, too, is one River of the life and power that comes from the flowing of the Holy Spirit.

## Prophecy of Streams Coming Together

Spiritual mothers and fathers, pioneers and generals are important in every move of God. There must be established voices that guide the flock and manage what the Lord is doing. That said, when you only hear from the same few voices for decades, and there is no diversity or variety of expression in what is being heard from God, you will be seriously lacking. The Lord is bringing back cross-pollination in the Body of Christ. With this, you will see a merging of the spiritual streams.

God said to me in a word about the streams coming together that denominational walls will fall among the evangelical and charismatic churches. In addition, there will be a mass exodus from the restricting and controlling traditions of man. As the streams begin to merge, you will see the most unlikely companies of people merge for the sake of the Gospel and a move of God. Those with different teaching and preaching styles are about to come together to accomplish the work of the ministry. You will see people who are heavy into teaching join forces with people who are heavy into the demonstration of the gifts.

This merging of the streams must take place to fill the voids and deficiencies that we now see in the current prophetic and apostolic movement. As great as the movement has been, and as much the Lord has used it to pioneer an age of the Kingdom, there is much still lacking. Many believers have gone to their corners and worshiped among their own tribe. But the day is coming where the tribes will come together so that the agenda of Christ might be accomplished in the earth.

Further, the Holy Spirit said to me that we will see cultural and racial barriers broken down within the Church. There is coming a move of God that will transcend race, culture, politics and the like. We will step into years of great unity among God's remnant. As I quoted at this chapter's beginning, Ephesians 4:13 talks about our attaining "unity in the faith and in the knowledge of the Son of God and become mature, attaining to the whole measure of the fullness of Christ" (NIV). God is calling for His Bride to come into the measure of the fullness of Christ. This will take a maturation process—periods of cleansing, pruning and refining—but it will come, and the Church will see an authentic unity like we have never seen before.

### The Racial Stronghold

The racial stronghold and battle in the United States has been intense. I believe God has allowed these issues to be unearthed to bring us into alignment with Him. Although unity will come to the remnant of God's Church, that goal of unity will not be met without enormous challenges. I see the principality of racism rearing its ugly head in the coming years again. This stronghold will be exposed even in the Church, and we will see the love of God poured out through the hearts of His people in response.

I have had the honor of pastoring a church and overseeing a ministry comprised of many races and nationalities. It is a beautiful thing to see the different cultures and races worshiping the Lord together in unity. This should not be a rare occurrence, however, or be seen only in a few churches. This should be the norm.

The institution of the Church has had an intense up-and-down battle with this spirit of racism. You can find this spirit at work all over the world, but in America, it goes all the way back to the origin of slavery. At that time, some people twisted Christian doctrine in this country to condone the most heinous crimes against Black people. Unfortunately, the institution of the Church played her part in racism in those difficult days.

Although many here have repented of this, the effects of the stronghold have often remained. Why is that? Because the first stage of repentance from wrongdoing is genuine remorse and asking for forgiveness, but the next phase is a complete changing of the mind and the thinking. Some of the old thinking still needs to change. In the coming years, we are about to see God completely renovate the minds of His leaders and congregations. He will break down the barriers that allow some people's minds to be influenced by the effects of what has happened in the past.

The battle involved with this stronghold of racism has moved from hatred and superiority over others to complete indifference. It has been the preferences of the masses that have kept us divided. We more easily hang with those who look like us and sound like us, because it feels familiar. We gather with the same types of people as us because it feels comfortable. Many people don't want the challenge that comes with facing and embracing the differences. But if we can take on the challenge, we can reap the beautiful benefits of oneness.

The next big revival and move of God is coming with Black, White, Asian, Hispanic, Native American, East Indian and every other culture and race you can imagine, hand in hand. It is imperative that we don't block out color and say things like, "I don't see a person's color." Color should be seen, loved and embraced as a beautiful difference between us because God made us all who we are. It is the coming together of all of the colors of humanity that reflects the image of God.

## Unity of the Faith

When Ephesians 4:13 speaks about the unity of the faith in the fullness of Jesus Christ, it is referring to a pure and mature Body of believers. It is referring to a Church without blemish. Because we have seen so much infighting and disputing over minor doctrinal issues, some people don't believe it is possible to unify. But it is not only possible; it is inevitable. The state and condition of the world will demand that the Church come together. As we experience the advancement of wicked agendas and immorality in the world, the principal thing becomes more and more important—and that is our faith in the Lord Jesus Christ. He is the only hope for the world. He is the only hope for the current political corruption. He is the saving grace for all of humanity's problems.

*Unity* in the Greek language means "oneness," and Greek was the original language Ephesians 4:13 was written in. Unity does not mean that everyone agrees on every little thing. Unity means that we all agree on the foundational tenets of the Christian faith. True unity is the maturity to say, "I don't agree with you on this issue, but I stand with you in the Lord Jesus Christ."

The bond of unity is covenant. Covenant is the greatest commitment there is. In the Old Testament, God made covenants with Abraham, Moses and David, among others. The term originally related to cutting. In ancient times, when someone would come into covenant with another, it was called "cutting covenant." These agreements often called for the cutting of the flesh and the joining or mixing of blood, signifying that the two had become one. This shows that real covenant requires sacrifice. God is bringing back an understanding of the true value of covenant relationships within the Body of Christ. It will require us to sacrifice, but it will bring about a great revival in the Church when we join together.

In Amos 3:3 the author asks the question, "Can two walk together, unless they are agreed?" Walking together around any cause requires a high level of agreement. The word *agreed* in this verse is the Hebrew word *ya'ad*, which means "to meet (at a specific time), to engage, to have an appointment or to summon." All God is requiring of us concerning the concept of unity is that we meet. In spite of differing opinions and varying streams, we have to meet.

Prophetically speaking, the Lord showed me many gatherings and meetings that will come into being for the sole purpose of uniting the Church. Many believers have complained that they have met with others from different streams, but that they have not seen success in unifying. Some say unity still has not come. But I heard the Holy Spirit say to me, *Don't stop meeting. It is through meeting and coming together that correction, proper alignment and covenant are forged.* In the coming days, we will see the spirit of unity/

oneness spread. It will be a beautiful sign that Jesus is coming back for His Bride, the Church.

 **YOUR PROPHETIC FORECAST**

Streams are merging, and God is causing a convergence to take place in the Spirit. Cross-pollination is part of His design. We can look to nature to show us how easy and natural it is to align with those who are different from us. Look at how naturally streams flow together into one larger body of water. This is a symbol of how the Church's different streams will come into alignment with one another. Just because it is natural, however, does not mean it is comfortable. God's Kingdom is diverse. It is the plan of the Lord to connect a diverse Body of believers together. You have an opportunity to be a bridge and a connector. You have an opportunity to be part of this great convergence. Here is how you can personally be involved with this movement of God:

1. Break out of your comfort zone. Be willing to talk to, fellowship with and communicate with other people who do not look, sound or even think like you. You will find growth in the differences.
2. Release prejudice and preconceived ideas about others. This is so important. When you prejudge others, you limit the benefits of what God can do through relationships with them. Prejudice is an enemy of progress.
3. Heal quickly from hatred, offense and anything that stands in the way of the move of God. The more you

are whole and well, the more God will use you to impact others positively.

4. Celebrate the difference in other people and recognize the need to draw from them.

5. Embrace other cultures and races in the Body of Christ. Don't view yourself as above or better. See the diversity among you, just as the tribes of Israel differed in their strengths, functions and specialties.

As you apply these points to your life, you will discover God's Kingdom in the most unexpected people. You will experience the convergence of anointings, wisdom and the collective power of unity through Jesus Christ.

 **PROPHETIC HOPE**

Walls of division are coming down, and you will see the glory of God bring about unity. Unity will be the driving force of believers in the coming days. This will not be false unity or a worldly uniting around a simple cause; this will be the unity of shared faith in the Lord Jesus Christ. You will see God connect the most diverse people for Kingdom purposes. You will see unlikely partnerships that bear much fruit. Even in your family, God will bring restoration and unity in a greater way. True unity in the Spirit is the doorway for massive signs, wonders and miracles to erupt.

# 18

# Global Reset

> The earth was formless and void or a waste and emptiness,
> and darkness was upon the face of the deep [primeval ocean
> that covered the unformed earth]. The Spirit of God was
> moving (hovering, brooding) over the face of the waters.
>
> Genesis 1:2 AMP

What is a *reset*? It is defined as "an act or instance of setting,
adjusting, or fixing something in a new or different way"[1]
to cause it to enter a period of reconstruction. If you think
about the term *reset* as it relates to your laptop or iPhone,
it makes it more understandable. If you have ever had to
reset your smartphone, typically all of the settings, apps or
programming that you have arranged are no longer there.
The phone goes back to the bare factory settings.

It is very similar when God refers to a reset in the world, or
even in your personal life. It is a period of deconstruction. To
deconstruct is to reduce something to its base components

in order to reinterpret or reshape it. When God allows a reset, He is inevitably allowing a pruning or reduction period, which means that spiritually a reset season may not feel comfortable. It can often be shrouded in what looks like chaos, upheaval and disorder. God often does His best work in the dark, however.

Let's take a look at Genesis 1, where it is already clear that the earth itself has gone through several resets. I just quoted verse 2, which gives us the perfect imagery of the condition of the earth at that time. There was emptiness. There was nothingness. There was deep darkness. It is safe to presume that the condition of the earth was in complete disorder. But the best part of the verse is that the Spirit moved over the face of the deep. The word *moved* here is the Hebrew word *rachaph*, which means "to flutter, shake and hover." This gives the picture of a mother hen sitting on her eggs, providing the right environment for their incubation. After a process and period of the hen hovering over her eggs, they hatch, giving birth to new life. Again, the Holy Spirit does His best work in the dark, when things seem to be in chaos and disorder.

Then the very next verse says, "And God said, 'Let there be light'; and there was light" (verse 3 AMP). The phrase *let there be* is not a phrase used in the Hebrew language for creating something. It is the word *hayah*, meaning "to exist, become or come to pass." It is not used here to create light. Light had already been created. It is used here to give permission for light to exist in this realm or context. It implies that it is possible that light could have been in that space before, and that God was allowing it again. It is possible that the earth was being reset.

There is so much concerning Genesis chapter 1 that is a mystery, yet it is possible that its verses pass through large portions of time. In Genesis 1:28 (KJV) God says to Adam and Eve, "Be fruitful, and multiply, and replenish the earth, and subdue it." The most interesting word in this verse is *replenish*. In modern English, this word means "to fill something up again or to restore." Scholars and experts debate over this word. Some say it did not have the same meaning at the time of the King James Version translation and that it only means "to fill." Others study this wording and see it as having the essence of the word *restore*, giving the implication that something was there beforehand. I believe it is highly possible that this word does carry the meaning of restore. God will often use a deconstruction period to usher in a new thing in the earth. It is my belief that God chose Adam and Eve to restore the earth after a reset period.

Now, I realize that there is much debate surrounding different creationist theories. As I said, scholars debate over the very meaning of the words used in Genesis to describe the Creation event. There is no way to prove any of the various theories conclusively, and it is not even important that we do so this side of eternity. What we do know for certain is that God created the heavens and the earth by the power of His voice. The timing, as well as what may have gone on before, is simply interesting to think about.

Prophetically speaking, we can also see that every new era and age in the earth is triggered by a reset. There are often many phases to a reset, and various components that make up its process. We are currently seeing a reset in the world on a massive, global scale. There is also a demonic agenda for a world reset, where wicked people in high places have devised plans to push wayward, man-made agendas. This is no surprise. Satan will always try to copy God's authentic plan.

I find that many Christians are so distracted by the devil's demonic reset agenda that they are unable to see God's dynamic reset agenda. It is time to put our eyes on heaven's agenda. God is resetting His Church, His people and every system of the world. Although we will continue to see calamity and unusual happenings within the earth, this time that we live in will be one of the greatest times of the outpouring of God's Spirit.

## A Reset Leads to a Fresh Start

When God institutes a reset, it leads to a fresh start. If you are reading this, you need to know that God is giving you a fresh start. You have a blank canvas on which to walk in the fullness of the dreams and visions He has given you. The current reset is just the doorway to your next chapter. The world's reset in every system, industry and sector is an opportunity for you to get in on the ground floor of systems that are being rebuilt. This is a period when you will see a major overhaul and reconstruction everywhere around us. And when any system is under reconstruction, the barriers to entry are lowered drastically and you gain easier entrance.

For example, if you wanted to get into the business world with government contracts, there are more opportunities now than ever to start your business and create a product. There are programs to help, and even grants for start-up funding. The Lord said to me that in the coming months and years we will see many people leave the careers and industries that they have been in for many years, and they will break ground into new territories for their work and business.

This time of major reset will unlock mega doors for you, and you will enter them with ease. In fact, this reset will be a fresh start for all of us as believers. Hosea 14:4–6 says in *The Message* Bible,

I will heal their waywardness. I will love them lavishly. My anger is played out. I will make a fresh start with Israel. He'll burst into bloom like a crocus in the spring. He'll put down deep oak tree roots, he'll become a forest of oaks! He'll become splendid—like a giant sequoia, his fragrance like a grove of cedars! Those who live near him will be blessed by him, be blessed and prosper like golden grain.

A fresh start comes with new pathways, new ideas, new places and even new connections. When God gives you a fresh start, it is a clean slate to begin again. This reset is a divine tool to give you a new beginning. If you can see past the discomfort, sudden changes and volatility in the world, you can see that God is opening a new chapter for you. But to fully embrace the reset, you must allow God to renew your mind and open up your understanding to the new things that are occurring. This requires repentance. The word *repent* means "to change your mind." It is a militaristic term that means to do an about-face, to turn in the opposite direction. This is the only way that you can embrace God's newness and progress in this season.

## YOUR PROPHETIC FORECAST

God is resetting your mind. Your paradigm has to shift in order for you to understand the magnitude of what God is doing in this season for you. A paradigm shift is a fundamental change in your methodology and approach. God is changing your mind in order to help you accomplish His purpose. God is resetting your *thinking, methods, imagination, perception* and *behaviors*. Let's look at what this means more specifically in each of these areas.

215

*Thinking*—The way you have previously thought (your mind-set/mental faculty) has brought you to this place in your life. It cannot, however, take you to the next dimension of life. When you want to go higher or make progress, you must change your thinking. Your thoughts are the vehicle either to move you forward or cause you to regress. Isaiah 60:1 says, "Arise, shine; for your light has come! And the glory of the Lord is risen upon you." In the Amplified version, it says arise "to a new life." This means to elevate your thinking. Your thinking holds the key to your future. You change your thinking by changing what you put before your eyes and what you allow to enter your ears. As Proverbs 23:7 says, "for as he [or any person] thinks in his heart, so is he." The word *thinks* there in Hebrew is *sha'ar*, meaning "gate or door" in its original sense. It means "to open." Whatever you open the gate of your heart/mind to, that is what you will be.

*Methods*—Your methods refer to the way you have been doing life. Everyone has a system or routine to the way they live their life. A routine can either create a foundation for success, or it can put you in a rut where you may feel stuck. As you seek the Lord, He will give you new methodologies for your life.

*Imagination*—Your mind is being renewed to capture and see imagery inspired by God. When God resets your imagination, He gives you creativity, innovation and pure thoughts. The human imagination is one of the greatest gifts God has given us. When we know how to properly utilize this gift, it serves as a gateway into the intelligence and wisdom that the Holy Spirit wants to share with us. Your purified imagination is your passport to dream again.

*Perception*—Your perception is the way you view or understand something. Sometimes, when life throws a curve ball in the form of circumstances, trials and trauma, it can damage your perception. Through the precious gift of the Holy Spirit, God repairs and heals the fractures of broken perceptions.

*Behaviors*—Our actions result in how we think and what believe. When the Lord wants to reset your behaviors, it starts in your mind. Character is the core of human behavior. The ultimate goal of any believer should be for his or her behavior to align with the core values of Jesus Christ. By hiding the Word of God in your heart, you can be transformed.

## PROPHETIC HOPE

After God resets you, you will be shot forth like an arrow into your God-given assignment. A reset is intended to bring you back to your original purpose and mandate. You will experience the renewing power of God as He repairs broken areas in your soul and restores you. Furthermore, God will cause you to recover all you have lost. As you have gone through trials and troubles, you may have experienced losses, but in this season you will fully recover them. You will see God restore your dreams, desires, opportunities and relationships.

19

# A New Kind of War

And you will hear of wars and rumors of wars. See that you are not alarmed, for this must take place, but the end is not yet.

Matthew 24:6 ESV

One of the signs of the times is hearing of "wars and rumors of wars." I have heard many people recite this verse and only focus on the rumors part of the text. But it also says you will hear of actual wars. War has been part of human history going all the way back to ancient times. People have warred for land. Nations have warred against one another because some of them have assumed that it is their right to rule. We have seen and read about wars over oil and other precious commodities. In recent years, there have been rumors of wars over threats to airspace and infringement of territory. Traditionally, when countries go to war, they declare or announce it, and they deploy soldiers and redirect their resources for the fight.

God spoke a strong word of warning to me for this decade and the coming years regarding war. Unfortunately, there is no nice way to relate what He said. It is sobering and concerning, and it requires our Spirit-filled intercession. He told me, *The new era will bring about an intensifying of rumors of war and wars within the nations. For there is a sinister plot of the enemy brewing to bring America and other nations into a years-long war that would cause great devastation and another blow to the economy.*

At the time that God shared this with me, He also said, *Mobilize teams of intercessors to pray for America and the nations.* This is something I have done and will continue doing. Before I go further into what the Holy Spirit has shown me concerning conflict and war, I want to reveal the purpose I have for sharing this. Yes, it is because God reveals His secret things to His servants the prophets. It is also the heart and desire of God for His prophets to come together in companies or groups to work in partnership as His intelligence agency in the earth.

## Prophetic Intelligence

In the natural, an intelligence agency is a government agency responsible for protecting and defending a specific country. Intelligence agencies collect, analyze and exploit information in support of national security, law enforcement, foreign policy objectives and the military.[1] Their methods can be quite scrupulous and aggressive. Their means of gathering information can be both covert and overt. These methods have been known to include communication interception, espionage, cryptanalysis and more. Intelligence agencies may provide the following services for their governments:[2]

- They give an early warning of impending danger, threat or crises to the nation.
- They engage in military intelligence by informing national defense planning and military operations.
- They operate in national and international crisis management. This includes helping discern the intentions of potential or current adversaries.
- They protect sensitive information and national secrets. In addition to protecting their own sources and activities, they protect those of other state agencies.
- They defend against the attempts and efforts of other national intelligence agencies. This is called counterintelligence.

Besides the points listed above, one of the main assignments of intelligence agencies is to covertly influence the outcome of events. This is done in favor of national interests or to influence national security.

What does all of this intelligence agency information have to do with anything? Spiritually, prophets and intercessors act as God's prophetic intelligence agency. At times, we pick up sensitive information through our prayer and our relationship with the Father, and we pass that information on to God's people. Then there are other times when God gives us heavenly assignments to pray and guard against spiritual intelligence information we have received. Those times are akin to covert operations, so the information is not broadcast to the public; rather, it is carefully covered in prayer by a congregation or group of intercessors. Then there are also times when we are given overt operations to carry out. This is where the plans and plots of the devil must be made known to the Church and world so that people can be made aware of his tactics and know how to fight against them. Being aware of his devices gives us the advantage, as 2 Corinthians 2:11 says: "Lest Satan should take advantage of us; for we are not ignorant of his devices."

Prophetic ministry, or as I call it, prophetic intelligence, comes to annihilate our ignorance of Satan's devices. This is the reason why the Lord would speak to believers who are His prophetic voices concerning future catastrophe, wars and the like. We are His agents who have the assignment to pray against the demonic plans that God makes us aware of, and sometimes to take action to counteract the enemy's devices. And for those things we cannot change, at the least we are called to prepare ourselves, and to prepare others in the Body of Christ for what lies ahead. With this in mind, I want to share more with you concerning what the Holy Spirit has shared with me about a new kind of war.

## A Different Kind of War

Of course, we know according to Ephesians 6:12 that we are in the midst of a great warfare that is not against flesh and blood. There are thrones, dominions, principalities and powers at play in the cosmos that are influencing and affecting the earth. This is the age-old spiritual battle that we see unfolding all around us daily. But in the natural, as God has revealed, there is a plot brewing. There are nations already at war, with a plan to secretly cripple the Western way of life and its access to comfort and convenience as we know it. The Bible is clear about a coming massive war of the ages, a battle that will be the culmination of things. Before that, however, we will see a spirit of war and conflict in the earth worse than what we have seen before.

The new kind of war we will see in the world will not be waged in old-fashioned battle lines, with artillery. The new kind of war will engage with artificial intelligence and will deploy nanotechnology and disruptions to technological systems. Data breeches and hacking are already happening, but these will become so frequent that they become the norm in developed nations and around the world. Some people feel that as long as they protect their personal data, these kinds of attacks will not affect them. What seems relatively harmless now, however, will in the years to come escalate quickly. Some of the world's largest companies and conglomerates will fall prey to cyberthefts and hacks that will cause millions of dollars in losses. In my time of prayer, the Lord showed me groups of cyberterrorists who will begin to arise, some of them backed by countries with their own evil agendas. Although cyberterrorism will increase, so will terrorism in the natural.

For many years now, I have prayed as the Lord leads, along with groups of intercessors in my ministry, for the United Sates and other nations. Several times, the Lord has spoken to me of a coming war that will be detrimental to the nation of America. In a vision from God, I saw three key nations (along with some others) band against America. I believe these nations have already come into a secret pact and agreement, and they desire to cause destruction. The result will be a different kind of war. They will use weaponry with advanced technology that has not yet been revealed to the masses. In this vision, I saw what looked like biochemical and cyberweapons, and even the use of pathogens. These rebellious nations have opened themselves up to be used of an ancient demonic principality called *Abaddon*. This is the destroying spirit that is now operating in the world. Revelation 9:11 (NIV) says of it, "They had as king over them the angel of the Abyss, whose name in Hebrew is Abaddon and in Greek is Apollyon (that is, Destroyer)."

During these times, it is imperative that believers come together to pray and speak life. The enemy desires to kill, steal and destroy, but God has given us the authority to declare and establish that life comes forth. Where there is darkness, we have the power to put a stop to or lessen the blow of the enemy's attacks. As a believer, you must always remember that your prayers are powerful, and that heaven hears your decrees.

Further, I saw that foreign entities will target the power grids of America and will seek to disrupt technology and electronics. In this vision, a major power grid was hacked, and millions were without power for a period of time. These are the kinds of attacks that the enemy desires to release. They are not the will or heart of God, which is why He would reveal them so that we might pray.

The Lord showed me a confederation and secret league between Russia and China that will bring disruption to the nations. This coming war will drag out for years and will mark a period of woes and tribulations. During this time, the Church will undergo great periods of persecution. Yet this same time of persecution will also mark one of the greatest outpourings of the Holy Spirit that the Church and world have ever seen.

### Israel and the Middle East

In the times to come, there will be much spiritual activity in the Middle East and Israel. Israel will increasingly become center stage for the eyes of the world. I saw a vision of what looked like a huge archangel standing in the midst of Israel, literally towering over the region. God said to me, *This is an angel of war*. And for a period of years in the vision, there was great warfare and battle over the airways above Israel. During this time, many ministers will be sent from near and far to minister to both Palestinians and Jews. An unlikely and unexpected alliance will form between sectors of Jews and Palestinians. They will begin to say, "We want peace!" Israel will experience a wave of outpouring, as many people will come to Christ.

I also heard the Lord say to me about Israel,

*At the time of Israel's greatest crisis in the coming years, an Esther will arise. She will come out of obscurity. People will ask, "Where did she come from?" I have sent her and anointed her to impact the destiny of the nation. She will break barriers and tradition, and she will arise to the highest office of the land. Yes! A woman will stand in the office of Prime Minister in Israel. And she will be raised up to save a people from great calamity.*

Furthermore, out of Israel will come great advancements in technology and weaponry. They will develop new types of defense systems in warfare. In addition, the Lord showed me a vision of a lab in Israel where they will be developing cures for some of the rarest forms of cancer. This brilliance will come forth by God's design. And in the years to come, cancer will almost become a thing of the past. As hard as that may be for some to believe, I heard God speak this to me clearly. With a simple pill, cancer will diminish. Israel will be key to this medical advancement.

## YOUR PROPHETIC FORECAST

This new era will be filled with conflict and wars. It is important that you remain grounded in the Lord and keep a sound mind. Remember, 2 Timothy 1:7 says, "For God has not given us a spirit of fear, but of power and of love and of a sound mind." God's immeasurable, unfailing love will be your comfort, and the power of the Holy Spirit will sustain you. So it is imperative that you guard your ear gates and your eye gates from anything that is contrary to the Word of God. Your ears and eyes are the gateway to your emotions, to your thinking and ultimately to your soul. Amid mounting warfare, you will have the peace of God that passes all understanding (see Philippians 4:6–7).

From a biblical perspective, here are some things you can do to navigate periods of spiritual warfare and even times of natural warfare:

1. *Discern or examine your path.* Ecclesiastes 7:14 says, "In the day of prosperity be joyful, but in the day of adversity consider: Surely God has appointed the one as well as the other . . ." The word *consider* here means "to discern." When adversity comes, take the time to think about and examine what your next step should be. In times of warfare, nothing should be done in haste.

2. *Trust in the Lord.* Proverbs 3:5–6 informs us that we must trust in the Lord with all our heart. When spiritual warfare arises, it takes faith to overcome such times of difficulty. Yet God has promised in this Scripture that if you trust in Him with your whole heart and don't rely on your own understanding, He will lead and direct your pathway.

3. *Be strong and courageous.* Joshua 1:9 (NASB) says, "Have I not commanded you? Be strong and courageous! Do not be terrified nor dismayed, for the

LORD your God is with you wherever you go." When terror is raging, pull on the strength of God. Don't fear! The Lord will never leave you. He will always be there with you.

 **PROPHETIC HOPE**

Daniel 7:27 says, "Then the kingdom and dominion, and the greatness of the kingdoms under the whole heaven, shall be given to the people, the saints of the Most High." God has given you the dominion and authority as you are seated with Christ in heavenly places. You have the victory. The end has already been written; it was established before the foundations of the earth. We, the saints of the Most High, win! No matter the conflict or tension we see in the world, we have already overcome the world because Jesus overcame the world. This is our declaration and our anchor of hope.

# 20

# Glory Awakening

For the earth will be filled with the knowledge of the glory
of the LORD, as the waters cover the sea.

Habakkuk 2:14

The Lord spoke these words to me: *We are entering into
the days of mega glory*. The glory of the Lord will fill the
earth. Glory is the breath, essence and atmosphere of heaven.
Glory is the substance and release that emanates from the
presence of God.

Over the past several years we have heard so much talk
about revival, and that is a great thing. But revival is just the
beginning of the move of God. Revival is for the Church, not
for the world. In order for someone to be revived, he or she
must first be alive, then be dead, then be brought back to
life. Revival comes to bring those who were once alive and
are no longer alive back to life.

After revival, however, comes reformation. Reformation is major change to the structure of an institution. God is reviving you and me and other believers, and restructuring our lives for the better, so that He can then release glory in our lives.

After that kind of reformation comes a massive awakening. An awakening is for the world and for those people who do not have a knowledge of Christ. It is those people waking up from a place of sleep or spiritual darkness. The only thing that can awaken people who are in the world is the glory of the Lord, shown through Jesus Christ.

## Eleven Types of Glory

The Hebrew language is so vast and three-dimensional that its words are expressed in images and pictures. Every Hebrew letter and word has corresponding imagery to better explain its meaning. It is often referred to as the language of creation. Hebrew is more of a concrete language, whereas English can be more of an abstract language. There are words in Hebrew that are difficult to translate into English. For instance, there are at least eleven Hebrew words for *glory*, which we will look at more closely in a moment. In English, we just translate most of them as *glory* or as an alternate word that does not embody their true meaning.

The Greek word for *glory* is *doxa*. It means "a state of existence." Anytime the Lord places a greater glory upon us, it brings us into a new state of existence, a new reality. Everyone does not live in the same spiritual reality. The spiritual reality we live in depends on what realm of glory we live in, or what level of glory we carry. It is the Father's desire that we move from one level of glory to the next level of glory. As 2 Corinthians 3:18 (KJV) says, "But we all, with open face beholding as in a glass the glory of the Lord, are changed into the same image from glory to glory, even as by the Spirit of the Lord."

The glory of the Lord is a transforming agent. It comes to unlock a deeper dimension of God in you. The more you experience the glory of the Lord, the more you become like Jesus. At a desperate point in the life of Moses, in essence he cried out, "Lord, we have seen Your judgment; now show me Your glory" (see Exodus 33:18). In desperation, the glory of the Lord was what Moses longed to see. God's glory is equal to His goodness and so much more. Here are eleven Hebrew words for *glory* that will help you understand what God is releasing upon your life:

1. *kabod*—This word is defined as "the riches, honor and abundance of God." It also can be defined as "a weight," because God's abundance is heavy and you must have the mental, emotional and spiritual capacity to carry it.

2. *hadarah*—This word means "the holy adornment of public worship, ornament and clothing." It is the glory of the Lord that decorates a person as he or she worships God.

3. *addereth*—This word is mostly known to signify "a mantle," but it also means "clock, splendor, a prophet's garment, and glory." The mantle of a prophet is the glory and splendor of the Lord.

4. *tiph'arah*—This word is defined as "splendor, beauty of garments and precious jewels." It is a glory that signifies rank and position. It is seen in Deuteronomy 26:19: "And that He will set you high above all nations which He has made, in praise, in name, and in honor,

and that you may be a holy people to the LORD your God, just as He has spoken." In this text, it is translated as *honor*, denoting the elevation of God's chosen people.

5. *halal*—This word is mainly used for praise. It means "to shine, flash forth light and praise." It is seen in Psalm 18:3: "I will call upon the LORD, who is worthy to be praised; so shall I be saved from my enemies." The name of the Lord brings forth light that is illumination and revelation in the form of glory.

6. *tohar*—This word for glory means "purification, purity and clearness." It is seen in Exodus 24:10: "And they saw the God of Israel. And there was under his feet as it were a paved work of sapphire stone, and it was like the very heavens in its clarity." Here, this word is used to describe the streets in heaven as being of such pure gold that they are translucent. This word for glory is connected to transparency. It is to be so clear that people can see God through you.

7. *shabach*—This is another word that we use simply as meaning "to praise or shout," but it means so much more than that. It is defined as "a loud tone, praise and glory." It is the glory that comes out of your mouth when you release praises to God.

8. *shekinah*—This is the tangible, visible manifestation of the glory of the Lord. It is glory that you can see, feel and interact with in the form of God's presence.

9. *hode*—Job 40:10 says, "Then adorn yourself with majesty and splendor, and array yourself with glory and beauty." This verse's word for glory means "splendor, majesty and vigor." This glory releases

230

not only the majesty of God, but also supernatural strength and health from God in the form of vigor.

10. *pa'ar*—Psalm 149:4 says, "For the LORD takes pleasure in His people; He will beautify the humble with salvation." *Pa'ar* means "to make beautiful." This glory is received through the doorway of salvation.

11. *tsabiy*—This word has the same general definitions as glory but can also be used negatively as pride. In the positive sense, however, it is further translated as "pleasant, or pleasant land."

## The Next Great Awakening

Matthew 4:16 says, "The people who sat in darkness have seen a great light, and upon those who sat in the region and shadow of death Light has dawned." This verse paints a picture of the next great awakening that is coming into the world. The eyes of many are about to come open to the saving, transforming and revolutionary power of the Lord Jesus Christ.

In the coming months and years, we will see and hear of the rise of more and more supernatural encounters with God. Many Muslims, Buddhists, atheists, agnostics, New Agers and the like are about to have mega encounters with Jesus Christ that will bring them into radical conversions. The Lord will appear to some of them in dreams or visions. Some of them will be at the point of death, and Jesus will completely raise them up and save their lives. Others will encounter believers in ordinary life who will be a witness and a testimony to point them to the Way.

You must remember that it is the Lord's desire that His glory be seen everywhere. According to Acts 2:17, where it quotes the prophet Joel, God wants to pour Himself out on everybody: "And it shall come to pass in the last days, says God, that I will pour out of My Spirit on all flesh; your sons and your daughters shall prophesy, your young men shall see visions, your old men shall dream dreams." The next great awakening will usher us into days of supernatural outpouring. Every generation will experience it. This is the word of the Lord that I heard for the next generations, which are rising in this hour:

> You will see My outpouring come upon Millennials and Gen Z'ers. They will be highlighted in the days ahead to be carriers of My glory. Many of them will prophesy accurately and carry of depth of My Spirit that the world has not yet seen. Some will ask, "Have the days of Smith Wigglesworth and Aimee McPherson returned?" No, this is not that day. This is an even greater day, where I will raise up a people that had no name and place My name upon them. And they shall carry the fire of My Spirit that will not be quenched.

## The Sound of Awakening

God showed me that a new sound will come forth even in the music in this new era. He told me plainly not to underestimate His ability to use secular artists. The hearts of people are in the hands of the Lord, and He changes them as He sees fit.

I saw in a vision secular artists being raised up after having supernatural encounters with the Lord. They will release the sound of heaven even under their secular music labels.

This is a day where we cannot afford to be bound by a false religious spirit, thinking that God cannot use whomever He desires. These men and women will be carrying the heart of God, which will bring freedom, hope and deliverance to a generation of people who would not come inside the four walls of a church.

## You Are a Glory Carrier

You are a glory carrier! You carry the heart and mind of God, if you are willing to avail yourself to the Father. He desires so strongly to commune, fellowship and partner with you in the earth to carry out His agenda.

The question is, Are you willing to be a transporter of the next move of God? Are you willing to show forth His glory to a world that is lost? If so, this is your time. You will be used by God greatly in the coming days to spread the Word and light of God everywhere you go.

To carry God's glory means that you house the presence and demonstrative power of God. When people see you, you have the opportunity to be a light in the midst of the darkness.

## YOUR PROPHETIC FORECAST

The glory awakening that we will experience in this new era will unlock a dimension of the Spirit that we have not yet seen. The gifts of the Spirit will intensify. God wants to use you to move in the gifts of the Spirit with ease and grace. His spiritual gifts will provide knowledge, wisdom and insight for navigating the difficult, yet amazing times that are ahead. Here are some signs of spiritual awakening to help you track the flow of the Spirit. You know you are experiencing a glory awakening when:

- You have a deep hunger and thirst for the Word and Spirit of God.
- You are being brought out of sin and demonic oppression.
- You have come to a new level of repentance from old works.
- You are sensitive to the interactions of the Holy Spirit.
- Christ is being formed in you again, and you are becoming more like Him.
- You are becoming a steward of revival in your own life.
- You are becoming a conduit to show the glory and goodness of God to others, that they may be drawn to Christ.

## PROPHETIC HOPE

You will see the glory of the Lord cover the earth as the waters cover the sea. You will see even more breakthroughs, deliverances, healings and visible manifestations of God's presence in the days ahead. Despite turbulence in the world, God is with us through it all. His Word is the lamp that guides us. His Spirit is the breath that sustains us. His wisdom helps us navigate new terrain. This is truly the greatest time to be alive and to be partnering with the Holy Spirit. God will use you to show forth His magnificent glory to others. You will be His glory carrier and the hands and feet of Jesus in the earth!

# NOTES

**Chapter 1 Architects of the Future**

1. I used the Blue Letter Bible's online lexicon as the source of all of my Hebrew definitions throughout this book, with the accompanying *Strong's Concordance* numbers that the lexicon provides for each word. For more on this, or to find out more about any particular Hebrew word that I define, visit https://www.blueletterbible.org/search.cfm#srchLexi.

**Chapter 2 A New Era**

1. For more on the earth's past time periods, see *Wikipedia*, s.v. "List of time periods," last modified August 21, 2021, https://en.wikipedia.org/wiki/List_of_time_periods.

2. For more on the definition of an era, see *Merriam-Webster* online, s.v. "era," https://unabridged.merriam-webster.com/unabridged/era.

**Chapter 3 A Shaking Is Here**

1. I used the Blue Letter Bible's online lexicon as the source of all of my Greek definitions throughout this book, with the accompanying *Strong's Concordance* numbers that the lexicon provides for each word. For more on this, or to find out more about any particular Greek word that I define, visit https://www.blueletterbible.org/search.cfm#srchLexi.

2. *Merriam-Webster* online, s.v. "promotion," https://www.merriam-webster.com/dictionary/promotion.

**Chapter 4 Issachar Arise**

1. For more on the meaning of *Tola*, see Nathan Moskowitz, "Tola the Judge: A New Midrashic Analysis," *jewishbible.org* vol. 43, no. 1,

2015, https://jbqnew.jewishbible.org/assets/Uploads/431/jbq_431_mos
kowitztola.pdf.

2. Ibid.

3. Ibid.

## Chapter 5 Nations and Kingdoms

1. The Traveling Team, "Needs of the World: What Is a People
Group?", thetravelingteam.org, ©2015, http://www.thetravelingteam
.org/articles/what-is-a-people-group.

2. *Merriam-Webster* online, s.v. "nation," https://www.merriam-web
ster.com/dictionary/nation.

## Chapter 6 Monetary Systems

1. For more on this, visit the Intelligent Economist's "Monetary System" page at https://www.intelligenteconomist.com/monetary-system
/#:~:text=A%20Monetary%20System%20is%20defined,treasury%2C%
20and%20other%20financial%20institutions.

2. "This Day in History, June 05: FDR takes United States off gold
standard," History.com, https://www.history.com/this-day-in-history
/fdr-takes-united-states-off-gold-standard.

## Chapter 7 The Days of Joseph Return

1. Israel Knohl, "Joseph and the Famine: The Story's Origins in Egyptian History," TheTorah.com, https://www.thetorah.com/article/joseph
-and-the-famine-the-storys-origins-in-egyptian-history.

2. Bible Study Tools, s.v. "Goshen" (Strong's H1657), https://www
.biblestudytools.com/lexicons/hebrew/kjv/goshen.html.

3. For more on this definition, see Dictionary.com, s.v. "economy,"
https://www.dictionary.com/browse/economy.

4. *Merriam-Webster* online, s.v. "harvest," https://www.merriam-web
ster.com/dictionary/harvest.

## Chapter 8 Technology Resurgence

1. For more on this definition, see Bible Study Tools, s.v. "paramuthia"
(Strong's G3889), https://www.biblestudytools.com/lexicons/greek/kjv
/paramuthia.html.

## Chapter 9 Unusual Weather Patterns

1. *New World Encyclopedia* online, s.v. "Mot (Semitic God)," https://
www.newworldencyclopedia.org/entry/Mot_(Semitic_god).

2. Bible Study Tools: Quick Reference Dictionary, s.v. "Euroclydon," https://www.biblestudytools.com/dictionary/euroclydon/.

3. *Merriam-Webster* online, s.v. "travail," https://www.merriam-web ster.com/dictionary/travail.

4. The information about lightning in this paragraph is drawn from National Geographic online, "Reference: Lightning, 5 Min. Read," https://www.nationalgeographic.com/environment/article/lightning.

## Chapter 13 Political Upheaval

1. *Merriam-Webster* online, s.v. "upheaval," https://www.merriam -webster.com/dictionary/upheaval#h1.

## Chapter 14 Judgment in the House of God

1. *Merriam-Webster* online, s.v. "punishment," https://unabridged .merriam-webster.com/unabridged/punishment.

## Chapter 16 The Underground Church

1. For more on these terms, see *Wikipedia*, s.v. "Underground church," last modified August 8, 2021, https://en.wikipedia.org/wiki/Underground _church.

## Chapter 18 Global Reset

1. Dictionary.com, s.v. "reset," https://www.dictionary.com/browse /reset.

## Chapter 19 A New Kind of War

1. For more on the role of intelligence agencies, visit https://www .cia.gov/.

2. For more on this, see the Federation of American Scientists Intel ligence Resource Program's article "The Role of Intelligence," https:// fas.org/irp/offdocs/int006.html.

**Joshua Giles** is an apostle, prophet and sought-after conference speaker. He has traveled to more than 35 nations in Africa, Europe and the Middle East. He is the lead pastor and founder of Kingdom Embassy Worship Center in Minneapolis, Minnesota, and founder of Joshua Giles Ministries and the Mantle Network. Joshua reaches out internationally through apostolic centers, prophetic schools and training modules, and he has been consulted by government officials, dignitaries and national leaders seeking prophetic counsel.

Further, Joshua is a media influencer and popular podcaster, with over a quarter of a million downloads and subscribers. His social media show *Global Prophetic Forecast* averages sixty to eighty thousand viewers weekly. He has been featured on national TV and media outlets, including the Christian Broadcasting Network (CBN), It's Supernatural! Network (ISN) and *Charisma* magazine.

Giles has a double bachelor's degree in business management and psychology, and a master's degree in theological studies. He has devoted his time to helping Christian entrepreneurs, training leaders and empowering believers. He has a great desire to help others succeed in what God has called them to do. More than anything, it is his ultimate desire to do the will of God for his life. To learn more about Joshua and his ministry, visit

www.joshuagiles.com
Facebook.com/ProphetJoshuaGiles
Instagram: @joshuagilesglobal

Printed in Great Britain
by Amazon